Criminal Justice
Recent Scholarship

Edited by
Nicholas P. Lovrich

A Series from LFB Scholarly

Capital Punishment in the U.S. States
Executing Social Inequality

Sarah N. Archibald

LFB Scholarly Publishing LLC
El Paso 2015

Library of Congress Cataloging-in-Publication Data

Library of Congress Cataloging-in-Publication Data

Archibald, Sarah N., 1977-
  Capital punishment in the U.S. states : executing social inequality /
Sarah N. Archibald.
     pages cm. -- (Criminal justice: recent scholarship)
  Includes bibliographical references and index.
  ISBN 978-1-59332-772-9 (hardcover : alk. paper)
  1. Capital punishment--United States--States. 2. Criminal justice,
Administration of--United States--States. 3. Discrimination in criminal
justice administration--United States--States. I. Title.
  HV8699.U5A8175 2015
  364.660973--dc 3
                                    2014038909

ISBN 978-1-59332-772-9

Manufactured in the United States of America.

Dedication

This book is dedicated to my husband, Dr. Zakaria Fatih and my son, Sami Fatih.

Table of Contents

List of Tables

List of Figures

Acknowledgements

I would like to thank the following people for their expertise and the insight they contributed to this study: Dr. Jeffrey Davis, Dr. Fred Pincus, Dr. Marvin Mandell, and Dr. Raymond Paternoster. I am also indebted to Dr. Marina Adler. Without Dr. Adler's support and guidance, I would not have completed the study that forms this book.

CHAPTER 1

Introduction

"The tendency to discuss the American death penalty as a national phenomenon overlooks what is in fact a sundry of state policies and practices" (Judith Randle in Sarat and Boulanger 2005:98).

In this book, I examine which political, economic, and social factors help explain the state-level variation in the adoption and implementation of the death penalty in the U.S. states in the last few decades. The modern era of death penalty legislation began in 1972 as a result of the findings in *Furman v. Georgia* (408 U.S. 238 (1972)).[1] This case nullified all 629 death sentences in effect at the time and commuted those prisoners' sentences to life in prison as a result of finding the death penalty statutes in the states to be unconstitutional. Although each Supreme Court Justice wrote their own opinion in this landmark case, Justice Brennan, concurring with the majority, concluded that the death penalty was inflicted so infrequently that its obvious arbitrariness was "inescapable" and that capital punishment in the United States "smacks of little more than a lottery system" (*Furman v. Georgia* 408 U.S. 238 (1972)).[2] Justice Brennan's statement had

---

[1] Please see Appendix A for capital offense by state and Appendix B for the dates of capital punishment enactments. These tables reflect the trends in death penalty legislation over the years since *Furman*.

[2] "The Justices in Furman repeatedly noted that the number of those actually sentenced to death represented only a tiny fraction of those eligible to be executed by the broad net cast by the state statutes at issue in the case" (Steiker and Steiker 1995: 365).

immediate implications for discussions of the death penalty across the country.

At first, many legal observers considered this ruling to be the end of capital punishment in the U.S. However, "[w]ithin two years of the decision, over thirty states had amended their [state criminal] statutes in an effort to address the concerns expressed in Furman" (Baldus et al. 1998:1649). Many states, including Texas, Virginia, and California, were quick to re-write their death penalty legislation. Other states either did not revise their statutes or did not have the death penalty to begin with, including Michigan, Vermont, and Hawaii. Some states either reinstated capital punishment after a long period without it, most notably New York, or imposed a moratorium on the practice, including Illinois and Maryland.[3] As usual, the Supreme Court did not provide guidance about how to proceed.

As a result, states have struggled to figure out whether or not to have capital punishment and, if they should, what specific form it should take. The only common underlying factor in current state statutes is that a person can only be put to death for capital murder, but each state has its own criterion as to what constitutes an act of violence punishable by death.[4] "In some policy areas the major cross-state

---

[3] New York attempted to reinstitute the death penalty after having done without it since 1976. However, it was ruled unconstitutional in 1994 in the case of *People v. Stephen LaValle*. Maryland's moratorium was brief. Governor Parris Glendening first imposed the moratorium in May of 2002. However, Governor Robert Ehrlich allowed the death penalty to resume in January of 2003. This allowed Maryland to execute Steven Oken in June of 2004 and Wesley Baker in December of 2005 (Maryland Citizens against The Death Penalty). In December 2008, the Maryland Death Penalty Commission recommended the abolition of the death penalty in Maryland. The Commission cited jurisdictional and racial disparities, in addition to costs, as a few reasons for its recommendation. The death penalty remains in effect in Maryland, although legislation was passed in 2009 to address some of the issues raised by the Maryland Death Penalty Commission. Illinois and Connecticut have repealed their death penalty statutes in 2011 and 2012, respectively.

[4] See Appendix C: Capital Offense by State, 2006 for state definitions of capital murder. It is important to note that Louisiana and North Carolina passed

difference occurs in implementation and not in the law" (Norrander 2000:773). Accordingly, I examine herein the adoption of death penalty statutes as well as the implementation of capital punishment, as it is measured by the total number of executions carried out for each state since its reinstitution in 1976 by *Gregg v. Georgia* (428 U.S. 153). Currently, Texas (482) and Virginia (109) lead the nation in the number of executions performed since 1972, while other states have not performed any or, if they did, executions have been relatively few, such as is the case in New Hampshire (1) and in Wyoming (1) (DPIC 2014).[5]

Because "[t]he death penalty is a political, moral, and emotional issue that cannot be resolved by the invocation of an axiom or by simple constitutional interpretation" (*Harvard Law Review* 2001: 1622), many factors must be taken into account to determine the place the death penalty has in today's society. Thus, it is important to outline this issue in a problem statement, highlight its relevance as a policy, and briefly analyze historical and legal changes in the United States.

PROBLEM STATEMENT

Historically speaking, states have implemented the death penalty to punish for all types of crimes. Over the last thirty years it has been increasingly touted as a way to get tough on crime and, more importantly, on dangerous criminals. The support for or opposition to capital punishment can bolster a political candidate's poll numbers or diminish their chances of election. In our highly politicized climate, however, death penalty implementation may not just be a community's logical response to heinous crime per se, but an indication of another

---

legislation allowing for someone convicted of raping a child to be sentenced to death. The Louisiana statute was recently argued before the U.S. Supreme Court in *Kennedy v. Louisiana,* No. 07-343. This statute was ruled unconstitutional in light of *Coker v. Georgia* (433 U.S. 584 (1977)). Coker was sentenced to death for raping a woman, an offense for which African American men were overwhelmingly executed. The Court found that the punishment was not proportionate to the crime, and therefore unconstitutional.

[5] These statistics are as of March 28, 2014.

more deeply rooted social problem – social inequality. [6] Racial, political, and economic factors have led middle- and upper-class Americans to have an elevated fear of crime, particularly as metropolitan areas become more racially and economically segregated and people become more politically divided. Unfortunately, the manipulation of crime statistics for political reasons has misled many average Americans and invoked in them unwarranted fear of crime victimization. The deceptive tactics have pressured policy makers into implementing increasingly strict and prejudicial legislation that specifically targets at risk populations, disproportionately affecting the poor and members of minority groups. Given these circumstances, it is highly important to examine the sociological, economic, and political variables that determine state-level variation in death penalty implementation. These variables may highlight other social problems which the death penalty is indirectly exacerbating or reveal that the death penalty is largely used as a mechanism for the social control of the disadvantaged. Consequently, this study addresses the following research questions:

1. What are some of the political, economic, and social factors that determine state-level variation in the number of executions between 1985 and 2009?
2. Is there an association between the number of executions and the political affiliation of the state legislature?
3. When controlling for political factors and demographic factors, is implementation of capital punishment a response to homicide rates?

POLICY RELEVANCE

The relevance of this study to capital punishment implementation is manifest in three areas. First, if the death penalty has been implemented

---

[6] This is not to imply that social inequality is the only cause of crime. However, numerous well-crafted and highly regarded criminological studies have found this link to be a strong one (see Blau and Blau 1982; Carroll and Jackson 1983; Patterson 1991; Fajnzylber, Lederman and Loayza 2002, to name only a few of the better known and frequently cited studies).

with the justification that it serves as a deterrent, the results in this study may either confirm or point to the contrary. For example, if executions are designed to discourage murderers, at a time when no correlation (or a positive correlation) between executions and homicide rates is found, this can arguably show that capital punishment does not deter murder. Second, if this policy is implemented out of fear of crime, yet the data show a correlation between executions and poverty rates, then this policy reflects the levels of poverty in states, as opposed to high crime rates. Finally, given that one of the responses stated for abolishing the death penalty was its unequal use as it is currently implemented, methods used in executions may be considered unconstitutional. While prisoners' and victims' race and poverty have been studied as correlates of the death penalty, other social inequality measures, such as the level of education of a particular state, exonerations, and its poverty rates, have not been included. As a result, several different levels of social inequality may be at play when it comes to the implementation of the death penalty.

The American justice system is plagued with problems of social inequality, and that also includes the execution of capital punishment. Mullin (1980:139) noted in this regard that "[d]eath row inmates represent a cognizable class of persons." She states that death row population has a disproportionate number of poor, young males and that these happen largely to be members of a "minority group" (Mullin 1980:139). Their victims tend to have a high social status, which usually means that the victim was white (Mullin 1980). Mullin (1980:141) also argues that with the murder of a high ranking white person, the community's immediate reaction is outrage, particularly since this "symbolic threat" disrupts the predictability of the lives of the community members. The reaction leads to fear of lower classes and seems to justify tougher penalties for infractions that threaten the *status quo*. Although this study examines state-level variables, it is important to understand the characteristics of the individuals who are being sent to death row and executed. Knowing who is punished can aid the extrapolation of which state-level variables may be predictive of the adoption and implementation of the death penalty.

The Death Penalty Information Center (2008a), among others, argues that it is not the depravity or gravity of the crime that most often determines the punishment, but rather "geography, race, gender, and access to adequate counsel" (see also Bright 1994:1836). Adequate counsel is often inaccessible to many capital defendants. According to Amnesty International (2008:5), "[n]inety-five percent of death row inmates cannot afford their own attorney." The lack of resources for indigent defendants strengthens the perception that "those without the capital get the punishment."[7] In addition, given that the victims of death row inmates are likely to be white, American society seems to place a higher value on the lives of Caucasians than on the lives of minority groups, particularly on the lives of African-Americans who are statistically at great risk of being murdered.

Reiman (2004:104) argues that the "criminal justice system effectively weeds out the well-to-do, so that at *the end of the road in prison*, the vast majority of those we find there come from the lower classes" (italics in the original). He states that the system does this first by considering what acts are to be criminal and what penalties meet each of those crimes; however, the same criminal justice system also continues to create exceptions for the wealthy by continuing to incarcerate and prosecute those from the lower classes. "At each step, from arresting to sentencing, the likelihood of being ignored or released or treated lightly by the system is greater the better off one is economically" (Reiman 2004:104). In the end, the image of jails and prisons are unrepresentative of the true nature of crime and punishment in America, since the poor are more likely to be treated harshly at each stage of the prosecutorial system than their middle- and upper-class counterparts (Reiman 2004). As a result, it is not that poor people commit more crimes, but that poor people are more likely to be punished more severely. As it is, the criminal justice system is not punishing for the criminal act, but gives the impression as though it is punishing the poor.

In addition, politics usually play a factor when it comes to the implementation of the death penalty. "Some of those who are guilty of criminal homicide but factually innocent of capital murder end up on death row because of a politically ambitious prosecutor, a lazy or angry jury, incompetent or over-worked defense counsel, or just bad luck" (Radelet and Bedau 1998: 111). Fleury-Steiner (2004) argues that this

---

[7] This quote is attributed to John Spenkelink, a convicted killer who was executed by the state of Florida in 1979

system runs the risk of devaluing life, since "the death penalty legitimizes inequality in the name of a privileged world-view based on the life experiences of jurors who have not experienced comparable marginality or disadvantage" (Fleury-Steiner 2004:135). As will be discussed, social inequality is a multi-faceted, multi-factored and deeply rooted social phenomenon in American society.

This book updates and expands the research on the factors that are correlated with executions of death row felons. This study incorporates variables that are noted in previous research (race, education, religion, homicide rates) while – in addition – testing other sociological variables that were either previously ignored or whose results have been mixed (exonerations, hate crime rates, multiplicative results of homicide rates and measures of race). Due to the complexity of the issues surrounding the death penalty, this study will expand our knowledge about state-level variation in legal system implementation of the death penalty and the number of executions carried out under state laws providing for capital offense punishment by death at the hands of the state.

OTHER ISSUES RELATED TO THE DEATH PENALTY

Besides social inequality, much of the research on the death penalty and the ensuing debate about it has focused on whether or not capital punishment is a deterrent, and what the costs of implementation are to carrying out this ultimate form of punishment. Because those issues have been thoroughly discussed in much of the recent research, the discussion presented here is limited to some key findings and lines of argument developed from these findings.

Deterrence versus Brutalization

According to the proponents of deterrence theory, people tend to attempt to maximize rewards while minimizing costs (Bailey and Peterson 1994). In the world of criminologists, there are two distinct types of deterrence – specific and general. Specific deterrence refers to incapacitating an individual to prevent him/her from re-offending. General deterrence occurs when a population is discouraged from committing a crime because the punishment (cost) is too great.

Deterrence theory also states that the punishment must be severe (i.e., that the cost outweighs the potential reward), certain, prompt, public and "applied with the proper judicial attitude" (Bailey 1974:417).[8] Since the modern death penalty system fails on many counts, some argue that the death penalty loses its deterrent effect. There is further argument over whether just having the death penalty serves as deterrence or whether executions must be carried out in order to deter potential murderers (Archer et al. 1983).

Some researchers and advocates argue that the death penalty actually has the opposite effect, that is, capital punishment actually increases crime rates, particularly murder rates. This argument holds that if people are exposed to violence, particularly government-initiated violence, the population will then assume that it is morally acceptable. This is often referred to as the "might makes right" argument (Bessler 1997). According to Weisbuch (1984:306), most of the literature supports brutalization theory and explicitly states that "street murder is not diminished by execution, it is stimulated" by it. Weisbuch (1984) also states that there are three ways that state-administered executions have a negative impact on public health. First, he found that all forms of social disorders, including homicide, increase following an execution. Second, capital punishment is expensive and uses resources that could be used for other programs, including crime prevention. Finally, capital punishment creates a conflict for those in the health profession who must work in correctional facilities where death sentences are carried out. By being part of the system, those professionals could potentially violate the ethical principles of their professional field (Weisbuch 1984).

---

[8] Hartung (1952) argues that the way capital punishment is carried out is contrary to the tenets of deterrence theory. He states that if a punishment is to have a deterrent effect, the population must witness it instead of it being witnessed by those who probably don't need to be deterred. In a similar vein, Reynolds (1977) finds that the presence of a death penalty statute does not necessarily guarantee that a murderer will be sentenced to death. Instead, according to Reynolds (1977), there is merely "an increase in the probability of receiving the death sentence from zero to some positive probability ([much] less than one)" (106).

The research is mixed when it comes to a deterrent effect or a brutalization effect (Clement 2002; Rubin 2002; Cloninger and Marcheini 2001; Radelet and Borg 2000; Sorenson et al. 1999; Bailey 1998; Harries and Cheatwood 1997; Beschle, 1997; Bailey and Peterson 1994; Cloninger 1992; Peterson and Bailey 1988). In fact, there are only a few studies that found that capital punishment has a deterrent effect.[9] Unfortunately, studies that attempt to prove or disprove the deterrent effect of capital punishment are difficult to design. It is almost impossible to determine whether the methods used are actually measuring deterrence, or if there are other unaccounted factors that are causing the presumed correlation. The time difference between conviction and execution, the intent of potential murderers, and sociological factors such as poverty and partisan politics may have an unknown influence on execution rates in general. Thus, there are too many potential factors to account for when attempting to measure the hypothesized deterrent and brutalization effects (Donohue and Wolfers 2005).

Some researchers point out that the abolition of capital punishment does not necessarily translate into higher murder rates (Radelet and Borg 2000; Archer et al. 1983; Zeisel 1976; Gerstein 1960; Schuessler 1952).[10] Despite ignoring most social science research that demonstrates that racial discrimination is widespread within the

---

[9] Apparently, not all methods of execution serve as a deterrent. Zimmerman (2006) found that the only form of execution that seemed to deter potential murderers is electrocution. In his study, Zimmerman (2006) reviewed state-level data from 1978-2000 in which he compared murder rates with the incidence of individual executions and the methods of the executions. Zimmerman (2006) did not find a significant correlation between other forms of execution (lethal injection, lethal gas, hanging, and firing squad) and the per capita murder rate.

[10] It should be noted that the Archer et al. (1983) study was based on data from European countries and did not include data from the United States. Radelet and Borg (2000) argue that increasing the severity of a punishment does not increase its deterrent effect, a realization that they state many scholars and citizens have come to over the last twenty years. These researchers go on to argue strongly that "capital punishment is not more effective than imprisonment in deterring murder" (Radelet and Borg 2000:45).

criminal justice system, the U.S. Supreme Court (under the White and Stewart pluralities) recognizes that the evidence is not entirely clear on the question of deterrence (*The Journal of Criminal Law and Criminology* 1976). The lack of evidence that capital punishment serves as a deterrent, and some convincing findings that show it might have the opposite effect (brutalization), has led the majority of leading criminologists to conclude that the death penalty does not deter crime (Radelet and Akers 1996). In fact, in a systematic survey two thirds responded that they felt that capital punishment had a brutalization effect on society (Radelet and Akers 1996). The criminologists overwhelmingly expressed the opinion that the death penalty does little, if anything, to curb violent crime and that it may actually increase it (Radelet and Akers 1996).

Unfortunately, the general public is more likely to believe non-repentant convicted murderers who state they would have been deterred from murdering someone if the death penalty was in place over the systematic, peer-reviewed research of social scientists. According to Galliher et al. (1992), movements to reinstate the death penalty in Oregon, Washington, Missouri, Arizona, and South Carolina were often energized by public statements of convicted murderers, individuals who claimed that they may have been deterred from committing murder if capital punishment was implemented at the time they committed their capital offenses.

Cost of Implementation

The cost of capital punishment has been employed by both opponents and proponents of the death penalty to strengthen their respective positions. Early arguments stated that it was cheaper to execute a prisoner than to lock them up for life. However, opponents of the death penalty argue that when all expenses – from initial costs related to trying the defendant to eventual executions – are taken into account, the death penalty is in fact substantially more expensive than lifetime imprisonment. In his editorial on the public health effects of the death penalty, Weisbuch (1984) estimates that the cost of the average capital case to tax payers was close to $1.5 million per case. Often the defendant is indigent, which adds to the taxpayers' costs because the costs of paying for both the defense and the prosecution have to be covered by the state (Weisbuch 1984). Additionally, when states need more funds to carry out an execution, instead of raising taxes, typically other social programs are left with a smaller budget (Weisbuch 1984).

Galliher and Galliher (1997) studied the cost of a limited death penalty bill in Kansas. Kansas has long had a death penalty statute on the books, but it has been extremely restricted in the types of crimes that can be punished by death. Galliher and Galliher (1997) found that the limitations written into the law would allow Kansas to keep costs down. In the first fiscal year, the limited death penalty bill would cost at most $800,000, with subsequent years resulting in even lower costs (Galliher and Galliher 1997).

Despite the high costs, strong supporters of capital punishment justify the costs (Radelet and Borg 2000). The proponents argue that the retributive benefits of the death penalty are incalculable and that no cost would deter them from supporting it (Radelet and Borg 2000). Bowers (1993) argues that as more research shows that each death penalty case costs at least one million dollars from start to finish, most Americans will be more likely to support a system of restitution. Such a system would require prisoners to work to earn money for their victims' families.[11] It is often argued that given the lack of a deterrent effect, other programs could be funded that may be more successful at reducing crime rates. There is no denying that the death penalty is an extremely expensive policy to maintain.[12]

---

[11] "Recent studies of death penalty costs reinforce the existing evidence that the death penalty is becoming unmanageably expensive. Like a black hole, it absorbs vast quantities of resources but emanates no light. Nevertheless, politicians and much of the public are drawn to it in the hope of finding a quick fix to the crime problem. But as the actual costs of capital punishment become clearer, the public should be in a better position to judge the death penalty as they would other [public] programs. If a program is highly cost-intensive, given to years of litigious expense, focused on only a few individuals, and produces no measurable results, then it should be replaced by better alternatives" (Dieter 1994a).

[12] According to Bright et al. (1995) many studies have found that a death sentence can cost three times as much as a life sentence, if not more.

This book examines the state-level factors contributing to the differential adoption and implementation of the death penalty in the American states. Chapter 2 outlines the historical events that had an effect on how capital punishment is adopted and generally implemented in the various states today. This historical overview is important in understanding the effects of the changing political landscape on capital punishment. The death penalty has been part of America's criminological history from the very beginning, but the methods of executions and reasons for retaining it have in fact changed over time. Within this historical context, a review of Supreme Court cases is important to not only appreciate the changes in capital punishment jurisprudence, but to note the social changes that led to the rulings as well.

This chapter also describes the role of public opinion, juries, and professional organizations in the death penalty system. While these entities are not the focus of this book, it is important to review historical developments in this area to contextualize the questions being posed here. Public opinion is often cited as a justification for implementation or repeal of legislation. Historically, juries were designed to allow the community to pass judgment on a fellow citizen, thus jury findings can arguably be an indication of society's values. However, given changes in the voting rights of those convicted of a crime, juries' decisions may not necessarily be representative of their communities' values. Also, juries that tend to be "death eligible," i.e., they would be willing to vote for a death sentence if they deemed it appropriate, tend to be more likely to pass on a conviction as well. In addition, professional organizations that have taken an official stance on the death penalty will be noted. The organizations have members that could potentially play a role in the death penalty process, whether it involves lawyers or anesthesiologists. Being the direct stake-holders that they are, it is important to highlight their position on this issue.

Chapter 3 outlines the relevant research published on the death penalty. This literature review covers political, criminological, and sociological factors as they relate to the implementation of the death penalty. The political section will include what role politics play in the process of adopting or repealing the death penalty. The racial factor section discusses the relationship between the death penalty and lynching which reflects the history of racism in this process. This section includes the effects of individual defendant's and victim's race on the administration of the death penalty, and highlights how these individual-level processes may be a reflection of state-level variations in values. While discussing criminological factors, the effect of crime rates on the implementation of the death penalty will be examined. Many proponents of the death penalty argue for the deterrent effect on murder rates and use it as a weapon to combat rising crime rates. Finally, studies on the problem of the frequent exoneration of innocent people who are incorrectly sentenced to death will be reviewed.

Chapter 4 outlines the theoretical framework for this study. Given that the death penalty seems to be influenced by a wide range of factors (political, economic, criminological, and sociological), this framework combines *Kingdon's Garbage Can Model* with sociological theories that describe the use of social controls in managing at-risk populations. The combination of these theories describes not only the process of adoption and implementation of the death penalty, but provide a context for its continued use, given the world's growing aversion to its implementation.

While Chapter 5 highlights the research questions and the hypotheses that will be tested in this study, Chapter 6 explains the proposed research design and methodology employed in this project. Specifically, bivariate and multivariate zero-inflated negative binomial regression models using panel data will be employed to study the six years covered by this work (1985, 1990, 1995, 2000, 2005, 2009). Each variable will be tested against whether the death penalty is adopted, and how often the death penalty is implemented (i.e., executions). Chapter 7 presents results of the analysis and Chapter 8 includes conclusions and policy recommendations.

CHAPTER 2

A Brief Social and Legal History of Capital Punishment in the U.S.

The first recorded execution in what would eventually become the United States occurred in 1608 when Captain George Kendall of Virginia was hanged for espionage (Reggio 1997). Contrary to popular media, executions were relatively rare in colonial America. According to Filler (1952), the colonies permitted the death penalty only for approximately one dozen crimes as opposed to over two hundred capital crimes in England. This fact is largely due to the rather small number of violent and property crimes being committed as a result of a prolonged labor shortage (Filler 1952). [13] Colonists had to work together to clear land, build homes and buildings, and establish towns and villages. The lack of resources and the need to establish colonies ensured that few people would commit crimes against their neighbors for fear of being left to fend for themselves against an inhospitable new world.

In addition to the fact that a more strict system of capital punishment could have been detrimental to the establishment of colonies, colonists felt that they should not be as strict and punitive as the system they left behind. Many came to the colonies to escape a system deemed unjust. This could explain the undercurrent of abolitionist feelings in the U.S. According to Mooney and Lee (1999a),

---

[13] "The Americans, however, actually applied the death penalty much less frequently than their British contemporaries. That may be because a greater need for able-bodied workers in the New World made wholesale executions impractical" (Atwell 2004:7).

there were three waves of abolitionism. The first wave began in 1846, when the death penalty was abolished in Michigan even before it became a state (Mooney and Lee 1999a; Filler 1952).[14] Rhode Island and Wisconsin quickly followed Michigan's lead respectively in 1852 and 1853, respectively (Barrows 1907; Filler 1952).

The second wave of abolitionism occurred between 1897 and 1914 when "five states abolished the death penalty" (Mooney and Lee 1999a:86).[15] However, as Mooney and Lee (1999a:86) note, death penalty policy "reinventions were contracting." By the 1920s, nineteen states adopted electrocution as their means of execution: Arkansas, California, Florida, Georgia, Indiana, Kentucky, Massachusetts, Nebraska, New Jersey, New York, North Carolina, Ohio, Oklahoma, Pennsylvania, South Carolina, Tennessee, Texas, Vermont, and Virginia (Bye 1926).[16]

The third wave of death penalty abolitionism occurred between 1957 and 1972 (Mooney and Lee 1999a:86). The numbers of executions steadily decreased until there were only 2 executions in 1966, 1 in 1967, and zero each year leading up to the Furman decision in 1972 (U.S. Department of Justice 2006a). The arbitrary

---

[14] The Quakers attempted to abolish the death penalty in Pennsylvania, but were only able to bring the executions within the walls of the prisons. (Quakers are "member[s] of the pacifist religious group officially known as the Religious Society of Friends that originated in England in the 17th century" (The Historical Society of Pennsylvania 2008).)

[15] In 1911 and 1913 Minnesota and Washington, respectively, repealed the death penalty (Filler 1952). Oregon, North Dakota, South Dakota, Arizona and Missouri would follow suit (Filler 1952). "Between 1917 and 1957, no state abolished the death penalty" (Amnesty International 2002).

[16] New York was the first to adopt electrocution as the state's means of execution. A heated public exchange began between Thomas Edison and George Westinghouse on whether William Kemmler would be executed using Westinghouse's alternating current or Edison's direct current. Edison's direct current was used to execute Kemmler. Edison felt that if Westinghouse's alternating current method was used, the public would view it as more dangerous and opt for Edison's direct method. For a complete history, see Essig, Mark (2004). *Edison and the Electric Chair: A Story of Light and Death.* Walker and Company.

implementation of capital punishment led the Supreme Court to rule that the death penalty was cruel and unusual punishment.

Another policy change in the majority of the other states was the requirement that executions take place away from public view. Although Kansas did not abolish the death penalty completely, it did put restrictions on capital punishment within its borders. The new statute required that the condemned criminal be incarcerated for one year before s/he is executed, and the punishment could "take place only upon the order of the executive [the Governor]" (Barrows 1907:181). According to Barrows (1907) no Governor had signed an executive order; as a result, no hangings were carried out. The Espy files show that only 17 executions were carried out in Kansas between 1853 and 1930 (Espy 2000). In addition, many states began to limit the types of crimes that were punishable by death (Barrows 1907). Many death penalty opponents were utilizing Cesare Beccaria's argument for proportionality, arguing that if a punishment is too harsh, the punishment will not serve as a deterrent (Blomberg and Lucken 2000). It follows that only the most heinous offenses should be punishable by death.

In his study of the death penalty at the turn of the 20th century, Barrows (1907) highlights five trends in capital punishment legislation: No state reinstituted capital punishment after abolishing it; the end of public executions; the change in method of execution; the reduction for offenses punishable by death; and abolition. These trends can be applied to the current state of capital punishment. With the exception of New York, most of the states that either repealed the death penalty, or did not have it to begin with, have not reinstituted it. In the late 1980s and early 1990s, there were calls for public executions via pay-per-view venues, but those proposals were quickly rejected. In an attempt to make the death penalty more humane, lethal injection was adopted by all states as the method of execution.[17] Although the offenses punishable by death have not decreased, those who can be executed (the mentally retarded and juveniles are now excluded) have been reduced. Finally, recent high profile exonerations have led states to place moratoria on capital punishment and, in some instances, to

---

[17] Charles Brooks, Jr. was executed in Texas in 1982, becoming the first inmate put to death using lethal injection.

attempt to abolish it. These trends appear to be repeating themselves more than 100 years after Barrows first published his article.

Despite the growing list of states following the abolitionist trend, many still determined that there was an apparent need to reform their criminal law statutes to allow for capital punishment. According to Filler (1952), this review was in part due to the U.S entering World War I. Tensions in America over the country's entry into World War I led to an increase in fear over other social problems, including crime. This allowed some states to adopt capital punishment statutes, while permitting others to reject repeals of their statutes. The Great Depression did little to alleviate these fears. Consequently, the 1930s saw the highest number of executions being carried out in the twentieth century, reaching a peak of 199 executions in 1935 (U.S. Department of Justice 2006a). During this period, however, states continued to modify their death penalty statutes.[18]

Georgia, New York, and North Carolina led the country in executions between 1930 and 1950 (Filler 1952; Hartung 1952). During this period, 3,029 executions were carried out; Georgia is credited with 280 executions, New York with 270, and North Carolina with 248 (Hartung 1952:14). In 1942 alone, of the 135 executions that were carried out, one-third "took place in these three states" (Filler 1952:135). On the other side of the spectrum, Idaho did not execute any condemned criminals, while New Hampshire and South Dakota only had one execution each (Hartung 1952).

As Figure 1 reflects, although executions are not as common as they were in the 1930s and 1940s, there was a steady increase in executions from the mid-1980s through the 1990s, reaching a peak in 2000. However, since 2001, the U.S. is again experiencing a decrease

---

[18] In 1919, Arizona, Missouri and Washington reinstated the death penalty, with Oregon following a year later (Bye 1926; Filler 1952). Kansas again attempted to actually implement capital punishment in 1935, but as of 1944 only three executions were carried out (Filler 1952). Like Kansas, South Dakota re-enacted the death penalty, but it was in name only. In 1939, that state reinstituted the sentence of capital punishment, but did not allow for funds to buy an electric chair (Filler 1952). The legislature attempted to rectify that problem in 1942, but there were no materials available to construct the chair (Filler 1952).

in the number of executions being carried out. This decline appears to have been set up by the redefinition of the issues surrounding the death penalty in the mid-1990s. According to Baumgartner, DeBoef, and Boydstun (2004), this redefinition went "from a focus on morality and constitutionality to charges that innocent people may be on death row and, later, a focus on charges of racial bias in the application of the death penalty" (Peffley and Hurwitz 2007:997).

Figure 1: U.S. Department of Justice, Bureau of Justice Statistics (2011).

Number of persons executed in the United States, 1930–2010

Executions

Source: BJS, National Prisoner Statistics Program.

Despite the decrease, it is important to note that states are far from consistent in their use of capital punishment. Ever since *Gregg v. Georgia* (428 U.S. 153 (1976)) allowed states to reopen their death chambers in 1976, 1299 executions have been carried out (Death Penalty Information Center (DPIC), 2012c).19 Of these, Texas has executed 482 prisoners, accounting for roughly 37% of the executions in the United States (DPIC 2011a). Virginia is a distant second, having carried out 109 executions since the reinstatement of capital punishment in that state (DPIC 2011a). As a region, the South leads the nation in executions. Since 1976, one thousand and sixty-five

---

19 These figures reflect executions up to June 25, 2012.

executions have been carried out in the South, thereby accounting for 82% of executions in the U.S. (DPIC 2014d). The Midwest carried out 12% of the nation's executions; the West has carried out 6%, and the Northeast has completed less than 1% (DPIC 2014d).

As Cohen (2003: X) notes, "justice is at best an inexact process. It depends on too many variables for it to function with precision: the quality of the defense attorneys, the intensity of the prosecution, the disposition of the judge, the reliability of witnesses, the makeup of a jury whose members rarely resemble the defendant's peers." In addition, "Norrander (2000) finds that current state death penalty policy must be understood as a result of a historical chain of factors, including not just the influence of current public opinion, but of longstanding previous policies and their effects, direct and indirect, on policy elites and the public" (Miller and Niven 2009:51).

Recently, even in jurisdictions that allow for capital punishment, there has been a shift in addressing concerns over the use of the death penalty cases that involve vulnerable populations, such as juveniles and the mentally retarded (American Bar Association 2003). There have also been concerns over the representation of indigent defendants and racial justice in capital cases (American Bar Association 2003). This trend was noticeable in 2001, 2002 and 2003 legislative sessions, during which time in "all of the 38 death penalty states, legislators introduced moratorium, abolition, or reform" (American Bar Association 2003).

LYNCHING

As noted previously, capital punishment is the most favored method and is used more often in the South than in any other region in the U.S. Many scholars and commentators have noted that this discrepancy between North and South is the direct result of the historical impact of slavery (Adams 2007; Gottschalk 2006; Atwell 2004; Bedau 2004; Zimring 2003; Lofquist 2001-2002; Nisbett and Cohen 1996). "Slavery does not, nor can it, just go away. It remains embedded as a function of law and other social institutions and, therefore, as a feature of U.S.

culture" (Adams 2007:8-9). Slavery was replaced with Jim Crow laws and lynchings[20] that were often left unpunished.[21]

According to his review of movements to abolish the death penalty in the U.S, Filler (1952) notes that Newton M. Curtis, a Civil War veteran and a reformer in New York, attempted to show that states with the greatest number of offenses punishable by death not only suffered from higher homicide rates, but also from large numbers of lynchings. With this information, Congress limited the number of offenses punishable by death to murder, rape, and treason (Filler 1952).

However, at the turn of the twentieth century, supporters of capital punishment, fueled by racial prejudice, argued that without capital punishment, vigilante justice would be committed in the form of lynchings (Cutler 1907). In his commentary on capital punishment, Cutler (1907) went so far as to equate whites with an "unreasonable

---

[20] "Lynching was a popular method of maintaining white supremacy within most states, especially within the Southern states. It has been estimated that on average, between 1880 and 1920, two African Americans per week were lynched. It was not until the 1850s that lynching took an extremely violent turn. Before 1850, victims were only beaten. After 1850, lynching took on the connotation used today. By 1890, lynch mobs took on another level of brutality, when the crowd began to dismember their black victims and sell their body parts as souvenirs. The most common methods for lynching included hanging and shooting, however there were more brutal methods utilized by white mobs, such as burning at the stake, maiming, dismemberment, castration, and physical torture" (Simon and Blaskovich 2002:61).

[21] "The term 'Jim Crow' was derived from a white minstrel character popular in the 1830s who mimicked the stereotypical characteristics of blacks – he sang and danced and acted as a simple-minded buffoon. Jim Crow laws passed in the South essentially attempted to erect a racial case system that physically separated whites from blacks. These laws required separate facilities for whites and blacks in transportation, education, housing, and other public accommodations. Signs that read "colored" and "whites only" were a constant reminder by Southern whites of the inferior social position of blacks and their second-class citizenship" " (Paternoster, Brame and Bacon 2008:172).

father" and blacks as "his child." He continued this racially charged dialogue by stating that since whites could not understand the motives of African Americans when committing heinous crimes, the punishments, such as being burned alive, were understandable and justified (Cutler 1907). Barrows (1907:178) reiterates this argument and states that public sentiment supports the "infliction of the death penalty" "both in the enactment of law [legal executions] and in the violation of law [lynchings]."

This alleged connection between the abolition of the death penalty and lynchings was the result of an increase in vigilante violence in Colorado in the late nineteenth century. Barrows (1907:178) noted that lynchings did not occur in Michigan, Rhode Island, Wisconsin and Maine, even though they were all abolitionist states. Hochkammer (1969) also found that this line of argument was dubious and asserts that there was not an increase in lynching in other states that abolished the death penalty. Hochkammer (1969) went on to highlight the fact that the South has had a long history of both capital punishment and lynchings, and there does not appear to be a correlation between the two. However, according to Galliher et al. (1992:574), "[l]ynchings emerged as the most important common triggering event in reinstatement of the death penalty. Significantly, lynchings occurred in each of the four states with the shortest periods of death penalty abolition."

In their book on the history of lynching in the U.S., Tolnay and Beck (1995) argue that the use of vigilante actions, particularly after the Civil War, was a way for whites to terrorize newly freed slaves into maintaining a similar system that had been present under slavery. They hypothesize that the increased competition for employment and land between whites and blacks resulted in resources becoming increasingly scarce for many whites (Tolnay and Beck 1995). Lynching was also used in the South to influence some political races, but politics were a minor issue when compared to the economic competition arising between the races (Tolnay and Beck 1995). However, Tolnay and Beck (1995:57) observe that there "was a perception by whites of a burgeoning crime problem among freedmen" (i.e., liberated slaves). It follows from these accounts of the post-Civil War period that lynching and the death penalty were both utilized in an attempt to neutralize a perceived threat to whites. Historically, that principal threat has been

African American men: "But the lynching of blacks by the white population was much more than just the punishment of a particular crime or even racial slight; the purpose was to create a climate of terror so uncompromising that blacks would be forced to adopt a position of timidity and inferiority they had known (and whites had enjoyed) under slavery" (Paternoster, Brame and Bacon 2008:177). What is particularly problematic about this period in the nation's history is that many of those who unlawfully executed African-Americans were public officials that were trusted to uphold the rule of law (Banner 2002).

U.S. SUPREME COURT CASES

The Supreme Court has weighed in on a variety of issues involving the death penalty. The Court's rulings have been anything but consistent, a fact which has led to the increasingly arbitrary manner in which capital punishment is implemented. The Supreme Court has attempted to follow society's "evolving standards of decency," but these putative standards are constantly changing as judged from the record of the Court (*Tropp v. Dulles* (356 U.S. 86 (1958)).[22] An analysis of capital punishment jurisprudence sheds light on the influence of the Supreme Court on the development of differing policies regarding the death penalty in the various states, where most prosecutions of capital offenses take place. There are eight overarching issues the Supreme Court has addressed in death penalty cases: cruel and unusual punishment, due process, juries and jury selection, aggravating and mitigating factors, mental illness, mental retardation, juvenile offenders, and racial discrimination.

---

[22] "In applying such 'evolving standards of decency' to the context of capital punishment, the Justices explained both that they detected an overwhelming societal consensus against the imposition of mandatory death sentences and that the 'fundamental respect for humanity underlying the Eighth Amendment' required consideration of 'the character and record of the individual offender and the circumstances of the particular offense as a constitutionally indispensable part of the process of inflicting the penalty of death'" (Steiker and Steiker 1995: 369).

Cruel and Unusual Punishment

Many defendants, particularly those on death row, have argued that their sentences violate their constitutional right against cruel and unusual punishment. Although not specifically defined by the Eighth Amendment, "federal and state courts have generally analyzed two aspects of punishment: the method and the amount" (*The Free Dictionary* 2008). In 1878 and again in 1890, the Supreme Court ruled on the constitutionality of specific forms of executions. In *Wilkerson v. Utah* (99 U.S. 130 (1878)), the defendant argued that execution by firing squad, the method used in Utah at that time, violated his Eighth Amendment right against cruel and unusual punishment. [23] The Supreme Court ruled that this method of execution was not cruel and unusual, but did note that "drawing and quartering, emboweling alive, beheading, public dissection, and burning alive and all other in the same line of...cruelty, are forbidden" (*Wilkerson v. Utah* (99 U.S. 130 (1878); Karge 1978:180).

Like Wilkerson, Kemmler argued that the new method of electrocution was cruel and unusual (*Re Kemmler* 136 U.S. 436 (1890)). The Court ruled against Kemmler stating that a defendant arguing that a punishment is cruel and unusual must provide more evidence "than the mere extinguishment of a human life" (Karge 1978:180).[24] A defendant appealing based on this argument must show that they are being tortured, or that their suffering is excessive.

Recently, some of Kentucky's condemned inmates attempted to argue that lethal injection was a cruel and unusual punishment in *Baze v. Rees*. The defendants' lawsuit claimed that the first drug in the three-drug cocktail used in lethal injections may paralyze the condemned inmate, but would not render him/her unconscious. As a direct consequence, the inmate would feel the excruciating pain of organ failure without the ability to alert officials of his/her plight. The

---

[23] In Utah, condemned inmates sentenced before March 15, 2004 have the option of choosing firing squad or lethal injection as the means of their executions (American Civil Liberties Union 2004).

[24] Kemmler became the first person to die in the electric chair on August 6, 1890.

Supreme Court ruled in April 2008 that the lethal injection method was not unconstitutional and executions using this method have resumed.

Although *Weems v. U.S.* (217 U.S. 349 (1910)) was not a capital case, it did set the standards for arguing against cruel and unusual punishment. The Court found that the sentence was disproportionate to the crime committed.[25] The Justices also determined that the definition of what is considered cruel and unusual is "subject to changing interpretations" (*Weems v. U.S.* (217 U.S. 349 (1910); Reggio 1997). For example, drawing and quartering was once considered an appropriate sentence, but this punishment has since been considered cruel and unusual under the Eighth Amendment by the U.S. Supreme Court.

In *Louisiana ex rel. Francis v. Resweber* (329 U.S. 459 (1947)), the Supreme Court ruled that Louisiana could carry out the death sentence on Willie Francis, even though local authorities had made one attempt and failed (Karge 1978; Reggio 1997). Francis' attorney argued that it was cruel and unusual punishment for authorities to have a second chance to carry out the sentence. The Court ruled against the defendant. The Court in *Tropp v. Dulles* (356 U.S. 86 (1958)) noted that in determining whether a punishment is cruel and unusual, we "must draw its meaning from the evolving standards of decency that mark the progress of a maturing society" (*Tropp v. Dulles* (356 U.S. 86 (1958); Reggio 1997).

As mentioned previously, *Furman v. Georgia* (408 U.S. 238 (1972)) struck down all death penalty statutes in the United States. The Supreme Court outlined four standards for determining whether a punishment was cruel and unusual. First, if the punishment was not proportionate to the crime committed, often referred to as the proportionality rule, then the punishment should be viewed as cruel and unusual (Reggio 1997). Second, if the punishment is imposed in a capricious and arbitrary fashion, it must be considered to be unconstitutional (Reggio 1997).[26] Third, the punishment would be in

---

[25] Weems had been sentenced to hard labor for embezzlement and falsifying official documents.

[26] "The Court's basis was that states were operating in too haphazard a fashion in deciding which defendants who committed homicides lived versus those who died. The Court concluded that the existing system had insufficient

violation of the Eighth Amendment if it "offends society's sense of justice" (Reggio 1997). Finally, if a lesser punishment would achieve the same effectiveness as the harsher punishment, then the harsher punishment would have to be deemed cruel and unusual (Reggio 1997). The Court found that the death penalty was implemented in such an arbitrary manner that there was little evidence that it was constitutional. The Court took note of the fact that there were few executions being carried out up until the time of this case, arguing that this was a reflection of the fact that the morality of capital punishment had been called into question on a broad scale (Steiker and Steiker 1995; Karge 1978:183). Although the majority did not rule that capital punishment was unconstitutional per se, Justice Blackmun felt that it would eventually be inclined to take that direction.[27]

The Supreme Court revisited proportionality in *Coker v. Georgia* (433 U.S. 584 (1977)). The Court reversed Coker's death sentence and found that death was a "disproportionate punishment for the rape of an adult woman" (*Coker v. Georgia* (433 U.S. 584 (1977); Karp 1978:1714). The Court argued that since the life of the victim is not taken, allowing states to put rapists to death would seem unfair, particularly when some murderers are not sentenced to death (Karp 1978).

In 1976, five cases were decided that would provide more guidance to the states as to what can pass constitutional muster – *Gregg v. Georgia* (428 U.S. 153 (1976), Proffitt v. Florida 96 S. Ct. 2960 (1976), Roberts v. Louisiana 96 S.Ct. 3001 (1976), Woodson v. North Carolina 96 S. Ct. 2978 (1976) and *Jurek v. Texas*, 96 S.Ct. 2950 (1976). These cases allowed the Supreme Court to rule that capital punishment in itself is not unconstitutional (Karge 1978). Grasmick et al. (1993) argues that Gregg allowed the criminal justice systems in the

---

procedural checks on sentences exercising discretion in making the ultimate life or death choice" (Bright et al. 1995).

[27] Chief Justice Berger, writing in dissent, states, "In rejecting Eighth Amendment attacks on particular modes of execution, the Court has more than once implicitly denied that capital punishment is impermissibly 'cruel' in the constitutional sense" (*Furman v. Georgia* 408 U.S. 238 (1972)). He notes that no Supreme Court decision has ever deemed capital punishment to be unconstitutional under the Eighth Amendment.

U.S. to become more punitive: "First, it opened the gates for states to inflict the death penalty; second, it ruled that public opinion was a legitimate basis for formulating justice policy (428 U.S. 184)" (Grasmick et al. 1993: 290).

The Georgia statute required a bifurcated jury, meaning that the jury would first determine whether the defendant is guilty or innocent; after that the jury would weigh mitigating and aggravating factors to determine the proper punishment (Fleming 1999). The statute also required a mandatory appeal to the State Supreme Court, which was designed to limit the arbitrariness that was found under the pre-*Furman* statutes (Fleming 1999). The Stewart plurality determined that since thirty-five states and the federal government had re-enacted the death penalty, then "contemporary values had not rejected the penalty" (*The Journal of Criminal Law and Criminology* 1976:438).

Louisiana and North Carolina had also rewritten their capital punishment statute, part of which required the imposition of a death sentence in certain circumstances (*Roberts v. Louisiana* 96 S.Ct. 3001 (1976) and *Woodson v. North Carolina* (96 S.Ct. 2978 (1976)). The Court again stressed the need for a bifurcated jury, thus striking down all mandatory death penalty statutes that were in force at the time (Karge 1978).

Due Process

Under the Fourteenth Amendment of the U.S. Constitution, all defendants have the right to due process. According to the Fifth Amendment, which applies to federal procedures, and the Fourteenth Amendment, which applies to state procedures, a defendant cannot be punished without first having a process that is not only free from arbitrariness, but one which also respects all the rights of the accused. As with the eighth amendment against cruel and unusual punishment, defendants have attempted to utilize this right in an effort to have their death sentences overturned. In 1932, the Supreme Court addressed the requirement of legal representation during criminal trials, particularly capital cases, in *Powell v. Alabama* (287 U.S. 45 (1932)) (Rankin

1979).[28] The four murder trials took only one day, and the defendants' lawyers did not confer with them to develop a defense. The Court overturned their sentences and sent the cases back for further proceedings upon finding that the youths were denied due process.

In *Patton v. State of Mississippi* (332 U.S. 463 (1948)), the defendant argued that he was denied due process since there were no African Americans on the jury despite the fact that there were members of this group qualified to serve on a jury. After reviewing evidence that showed that no African American had served on a jury in Lauderdale County for more than thirty years, the Supreme Court ruled that the County violated the defendant's right to Equal Protection under the Fourteenth Amendment (Rankin 1979:194). In *Fikes v. Alabama* (352 U.S. 191 (1957)), the Court examined a case involving a coerced confession.[29] The Court found that Fikes was denied due process as a result of his mental condition and the questioning of the defendant by authorities without legal counsel (*Fikes v. Alabama* 352 U.S. 191 (1957); Rankin 1979:194).

Juries and Jury Selection

The Supreme Court has attempted to outline how to convene an impartial jury, as required under the Constitution. In *Witherspoon v. Illinois* (391 U.S. 510 (1968)), the Supreme Court addressed the issue of jury selection. The Court found that the defendant's sixth amendment right to an impartial jury was violated because all who expressed opposition to the death penalty were dismissed by the prosecution (Rankin 1979:194). The Court did state that if a juror cannot impose the death penalty, he/she can be dismissed.

---

[28] Known as the "Scottsboro Boys," nine African American youths were tried, convicted and condemned to die for the rape of a white woman.

[29] Fikes was deemed to be either mentally ill or mentally retarded, but was convicted of rape and sentenced to death based on his two confessions while in police custody. Fikes had been in custody for five days without any contact with his family or his lawyer when he made his first confession. The police continued to question him and obtained another confession five days after the first.

The Supreme Court has ruled that a defendant has the right to question jurors about racial prejudice (*Turner v. Murray* 476 U.S. 28 (1986)). Justice White noted that the trial judge had discretion as to the types and numbers of questions asked of potential jury members and that special circumstances may require different types of questions.

Aggravating and Mitigating Factors

As mentioned previously, the Supreme Court not only required the bifurcation of juries to consider guilt and punishment separately, but also to weigh the mitigating factors of the defendant and aggravating factors of the crime. After their death penalty laws were struck down by the decision issued in *Furman*, Florida and Texas implemented a new statute that required the sentencing authority (in this case the trial judge) to explicitly weigh aggravating and mitigating factors. The Court upheld the convictions and the sentences based on the revised death penalty statute requirements that would limit the potential arbitrariness of death sentences (*Proffitt v. Florida* (96 S.Ct. 2960 (1976), *Jurek v. Texas* (96 S.Ct. 2950 (1976)).

The Supreme Court ruled that the use of depravity as an aggravating factor is not permitted *(Godfrey v. Georgia* 446 U.S. 420 (1980)) and that defendants should be given the opportunity to present evidence of their good behavior in prison as a mitigating factor (*Skipper v. South Carolina* 476 U.S. 1 (1986)).

Mental Illness and Mental Retardation

In *Ford v. Wainwright* (477 U.S. 399 (1986)) the Court found that execution of a mentally ill person is unconstitutional. Three reasons are provided by the Court for this ruling. First, allowing for the insane to be executed offends humanity (Dolinko 1986:552). Second, "it is cruel to execute someone with 'no capacity to come to grips with his own conscience or deity'" (Dolinko 1986:552). Finally, there is virtually no retributive value, since the person being executed is not consciously aware as to why he/she is being executed (Dolinko 1986:552).

Although the Court ruled on the execution of the mentally ill, it was not until *Penry v. Lynaugh* (492 U.S. 302 (1989)) that it addressed whether a mentally retarded person could be executed.[30] The Court ruled that the jury should have been apprised of his disability, but that even if Penry is retarded, he can still be executed.[31]

However, thirteen years later, the Supreme Court reversed itself. In *Atkins v. Virginia* (536 U.S. 304 (2002)), the Court ruled that executing the mentally retarded was cruel and unusual punishment, which violates the Eighth Amendment. In its ruling the Court highlighted the fact that eighteen states plus the federal government prohibited the execution of someone who is mentally retarded (DPIC 2007b). This reflects the "evolving standards of decency" in American society.

Juvenile Offenders

In 1987, the Supreme Court ruled that executing minors under the age of 16 is cruel and unusual punishment in *Thompson v. Oklahoma* (108 S. Ct. 2687 (1987)), again citing the "evolving standards of society" measure set out in *Tropp v. Dulles*.[32] In 2005, the Supreme Court was again asked to rule on the minimum age a person may be sentenced to death in *Roper v. Simmons* (543 U.S. 551 (2005)).[33] The Court found that the minimum age should now be set at 18 years of age. Those who argue against executing juveniles note that the defendant's age should

---

[30] Penry was a retarded man convicted and sentenced to death for murder. His mental ability was never taken into consideration as a mitigating factor at his sentencing.

[31] Please note that there is a difference between mental illness and mental retardation. Mental illness (or insanity) is defined as "Mental illness is a term used for a variety of disorders causing severe disturbances in thinking, feeling and relating to others. Persons suffering from mental illness have a substantially diminished capacity for coping with the ordinary demands of life" (U.S. Legal Definitions 2008a). Mental retardation is defined as "a genetic disorder manifested in significantly below average overall intellectual functioning and deficits in adaptive behavior" (U.S. Legal Definitions 2008b).

[32] The defendant was 15 at the time he murdered his allegedly abusive brother-in-law. He was tried as an adult and sentenced to death.

[33] The defendant had been convicted and sentenced to death for a murder he committed when he was 17.

speak to his/her culpability. Studies on hormonal changes and logical reasoning have found that despite the fact that adolescents may know right from wrong, they may not be able to control their urges to the same degree as adults (American Bar Association 2004). In addition, the U.S. Supreme Court decided that life sentences without the possibility of parole for juveniles are unconstitutional in *Miller v. Alabama* (567 U. S. ____ (2012)).[34]

Racial Discrimination

The Supreme Court took up the issue of racial discrimination in *McCleskey v. Kemp* (481 U.S. 279 (1987)). The defendant presented the Court with a study by Professor Baldus that showed that those who kill whites are statistically more likely to receive the death penalty. The Court dismissed his claim. Blume et al. (1998) argue that if the Court had reversed McCleskey's death sentence based on the evidence presented, potentially hundreds of other death sentences and convictions would have also been invalidated.

It is clear that the Supreme Court rulings have been marked by inconsistencies and contradictory rulings, rulings that sometimes had to do with the partisan political affiliations of judges within the Supreme Court. In addition, it is only recently that the Supreme Court has held that the *Bill of Rights* applies not just to proceedings in federal courts, but in state courts as well (G. King 2008). Several other groups have voiced their position on the issue of capital punishment, some of which have a direct role to play within the process.

PUBLIC OPINION

An important body of research regarding public opinion and the death penalty has emerged over the last century. However, the subject is complex and difficult to study, particularly because many Americans think about capital punishment only in abstract terms (Haney and Logan 1994: 83). Haddock and Zanna (1998) point out that just by

---

[34] "The Eighth Amendment forbids a sentencing scheme that mandates life in prison without possibility of parole for juvenile homicide offenders" (*Miller v. Alabama*).

asking one question about a person's opinion of the death penalty does not explain exactly what he/she thinks or feels about capital punishment.[35] This is an important issue, as Hochkammer (1969:368) aptly points out in his legal commentary when he says that no matter where the issue is ultimately settled, "the resolution will depend upon public opinion." In his sociological commentary after World War II, Deets (1948) expressed concern that unless a strong voice motivated public opinion, psychiatrists would continue to rationalize and explain the murder and death penalty trends in the U.S., thus resulting in a skewed version of what the statistics mean. However, it is important to consider the arguments on both sides of the death penalty debate.

Many articles outline the arguments for and against the death penalty. Reynolds (1977) demonstrates that there is a dichotomy in the American debate in his commentary, which covered the sociological and economic aspects of the death penalty. Americans want prisoners to be treated humanely, but they also want them to pay for their crimes. Reynolds (1977) notes that the acceptance of more humane treatment for prisoners is in part due to an increase in Americans' standard of living. With an increase in overall prosperity, society tends to become more prepared to administer more expensive and more humane forms of punishment (Reynolds 1977). However, as tougher times come along inequality grows, Americans are less likely to accept humane punishments and support more severe measures in an effort to exercise more control over the poor in this country.

In terms of public opinion polls and capital punishment, many studies have been conducted to determine what types of people are more likely to support the death penalty. In their 1982 survey of 200

---

[35] These researchers distributed one of two surveys to 161 students taking an introductory psychology course in Ontario, Canada. One survey balanced affective (i.e., feelings), cognitive (i.e., beliefs) and attitudinal measures of respondents' opinion of capital punishment, while the second survey required a completion of the attitudinal measures prior to completing the questions that measured affective and cognitive measures. These three measures accounted for 66% of the variance in the participants' responses to capital punishment. Since this is usually not stressed when public opinion polls are reported, policymakers may misunderstand or ignore public opinion (Haddock and Zanna 1998).

Illinois residents on opinions about the death penalty, Tyler and Weber (1982) found that political and social attitudes were strongly linked to the perceived value of deterrence, retribution, and humanitarianism. Nice (1992) examined data from the early to mid-1970s to determine what factors could predict individual views on the adoption and implementation of the death penalty and found that conservatives are more likely to support capital punishment than liberals. In the 1930s, research determined that there was also a strong relationship between public opinion and state death penalty policies (Nice 1992). Republican states tend to have "proportionally large death row populations" and high rates of murder and non-negligent manslaughter (Nice 1992:1042-1044). Finally, polls have shown that African Americans are less likely to support capital punishment than whites, and that wealthy people are more likely to support it than the poor (Unnever, Cullen, and Jonson 2008; Peffley and Hurwitz 2007; Unnever, Cullen, and Johnson 2008; Unnever and Cullen 2007; Cochran and Chamlin 2006; Unnever and Cullen 2005; Baumer, Messner, and Rosenfeld 2003; Soss, Langbein, and Metelko 2003; Nice 1992; Young 1991).

Support for the death penalty appears to be cyclical in nature. In her review of Gallup Polls, Erskine (1970) found that there was a decline in the support of capital punishment between 1936 and 1966, going from 62% to 42%. However, by 1969, the support of capital punishment had risen again to 51% (Erskine 1970). Erskine (1970:290) attributes this increase to the public's call "for law, order, and more severity in the judicial and penal system." A 1958 Roper Poll shows that people are not as certain about their support of the death penalty (Hochkammer 1969). Respondents were asked whether the worst criminals should receive death or life imprisonment; "42% favored the death penalty, 50% favored life imprisonment, and 8% were undecided" (Hochkammer 1969:364). Those numbers have changed slightly since the 1960s, as shown by Figure 2 below with 33% favoring the death penalty, 9% favoring life with parole, 13% favoring life without the possibility of parole, and 39% favoring life without the possibility of parole and restitution.

Figure 2: Public Opinion Poll – May 2010 (Death Penalty Information
Center 2012)

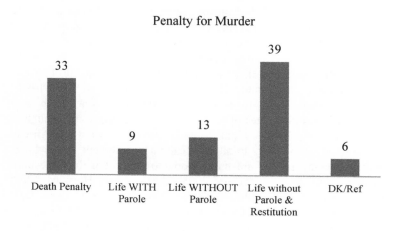

Penalty for Murder

In the 1990s, public support for capital punishment was generally
high, but not consistent across states. Rhode Island had the lowest level
of support at 61%, while Florida had the highest at 91% (Norrander
2000). However, Galliher and Galliher (1997) noted that Americans are
not as supportive of capital punishment when presented with other
options. The researchers gave respondents the choice between
supporting the death penalty and supporting life without the possibility
of parole in conjunction with restitution for victims' families. Support
for capital punishment "drops precipitously" when provided with this
other option (Galliher and Galliher 1997:370). Radelet and Borg (2000)
came to a similar conclusion in their analysis of death penalty debates,
particularly as Americans come to realize that life without the
possibility of parole does not allow for an early release.

Galliher and Galliher (1997) also note that even though a state or a
region has a capital punishment statute does not necessarily mean that
the citizenry there favors it. They observe that the whole South
currently has a much lower level of public support for the death penalty
than other regions despite the fact that the South leads the rest of the
nation in executions (Galliher and Galliher 1997).

It is important to note that public policy is generally affected by public opinion. In determining this impact, Burstein (2003) completed a meta-analysis of previous research. He found that "Public opinion affects policy three-quarters of the times its impact is gauged; its effect is of substantial policy importance at least a third of the time, and probably a fair amount more" (Burnstein 2003:36). Taking into account stakeholders, such as political organizations, salience and responsiveness of the issue often trump the attempts of the governing elite to shape public policy (Burnstein 2003). However, in terms of capital punishment it is doubtful that many political organizations or the governing elites would attempt to voice opposition to the death penalty when the majority of Americans persistently support it.

JURIES

The role of the jury in capital cases is important on various levels. First, the jury decides the guilt or innocence of the defendant. If the jury finds a defendant guilty, it must then decide between life imprisonment and death. Finally, juries' decisions have been used by state and federal courts to gauge public opinion, particularly since the jury should be comprised of members of the defendant's peers (Haney et al. 1994; Nice 1992; *Thompson v. Oklahoma,* 1988). Juries are an important part of the process because, as Mullin (1980:154) states, they "serve as symbolic indicators of our feelings about the poor and minorities, and of our true commitment to justice and equality."

The jury's role in life and death decisions has led a host of researchers to examine who is on a jury, how they make decisions, and how much they know about the criminal justice system. The Supreme Court has changed the guidelines as to who can be excluded from a jury on a capital case. In 1968, the U.S. Supreme Court first ruled that a juror can be constitutionally excluded if he/she expressed "unequivocal opposition" to capital punishment (*Witherspoon v. Illinois* 1968; Haney et al. 1994:619). However, the standard was changed from "unequivocal opposition" to merely holding death penalty attitudes that would "prevent or substantially impair the performance of his [or her] duties as a juror in accordance with his [or her] instructions and oath" (*Wainwright v. Witt* 477 U.S. 168 (1985); Haney et al. 1994:621). In 1992, the Court decided that potential jurors who would always impose the death penalty could be constitutionally excluded from the jury due to the fact that they could be assumed to be insufficiently impartial (*Morgan v. Illinois* 504 US 719 (1992); Haney et al. 1994).

These restrictions have taken place in a time when support for the death penalty is relatively high (Haney et al. 1994:622). According to researchers, this rise has led to a skewing in qualified jurors in terms of perceptions and attitudes, not to mention the increased probability of returning a guilty verdict (Robinson 1993; Luginbuhl and Kathi 1988; Carr 1987; Fitzgerald and Ellsworth 1984; Haney 1984). In his study on the subject of death qualified jurors and excludables, Robinson (1993) offered five grisly vignettes and asked subjects who would have been considered "excludable" whether they would impose the death penalty in those cases. "Death qualified jurors" tend to note that they are more concerned with crime control, and less worried about due process than excludables (Robinson 1993).[36] These jurors also are less regretful when it comes to convictions of the innocent (Robinson 1993). Robinson (1993) also notes that there is more debate when excludables are allowed on a jury, and that juries including excludables tend to recall facts better.[37] As with many studies, the subjects were recruited from an Introduction to Psychology course, thus resulting in an issue of whether the results would be generalizable to the rest of the American population.

According to Haney et al. (1994), excludable jurors who expressed opposition to the death penalty tended to be more liberal in their views (see also Butler and Moran 2002). These researchers conducted 498 telephone surveys with California residents. Their findings suggest that

---

[36] "Compared to the death-qualified jurors, the members of the excluded group are more concerned with the maintenance of the fundamental due process guarantees of the Constitution, less punitive, and less mistrustful of the defense" (Fitzgerald and Ellsworth 1984:46-48).

[37] In a similar vein, Luginbuhl and Kathi (1988:271) found that there was "a strong relationship between level of belief in the death penalty and acceptance of mitigating circumstances but no relationship between level of belief in the death penalty and acceptance of aggravating circumstances." They theorize that this might be the result of those who are firmly opposed to capital punishment taking into consideration all facts before coming to a decision.

these jurors are less inclined to believe that harsher treatments will affect crime, and more likely to think that the death penalty was more expensive than life imprisonment. Conversely, jurors who would be excluded as a result of their unequivocal support of the death penalty tend to have more conservative views than acceptable jurors and the other excludable jurors (Haney et al. 1994). The authors also found that excludable jurors were more inclined to believe in the deterrent effect of the death penalty and were less concerned with due process and equality within the criminal justice system.[38]

Jacoby and Paternoster (1982) collected data regarding murders from the South Carolina State Law Enforcement Division's Supplemental Homicide Reports for the period June 8, 1977 through November 30, 1979. Jury attitudes were measured using data from two telephone surveys that were conducted in September 1980 and October 1981. A random selection of registered voters was then asked about their thoughts on upcoming murder trials in their county. Jacoby and Paternoster (1982) found that death qualified jurors were more likely to feel that a defendant was guilty than excludable respondents. This is important to note in light of the fact that 54.2% of those who felt the defendant was innocent would have been excluded (Jacoby and Paternoster 1982).

Another potential problem with the current guidelines for excluding jurors is the underrepresentation of certain groups on capital juries. Under the *Witherspoon* exclusions, African Americans, less educated people, Jews, and agnostics are more likely to be excused from serving on a capital jury, which leads to decisions that may not represent what a community values (Jacoby and Paternoster 1982). In addition, jurors' names are drawn from voter and property owner lists, a sampling process which would cause a marked underrepresentation of "young people, women, blacks, Hispanics, Indians and the poor" (Mullin 1980:145).

---

[38] One potential drawback of this study is the sample. By limiting the potential subjects to one particular geographic area, it is difficult to generalize results to other populations. Historically, California has been more liberal than the rest of the country. As a consequence, the respondents' answers to capital punishment questions cannot necessarily predict how other respondents in states might respond on the same questions.

It is important to mention that jury members are likely to be recruited from the same sample used by Jacoby and Paternoster (1982), which allows for the responses to be used as evidence that the jury selection process is skewed. However, due to the geographic limitation, it is unclear whether this trend is evident nationwide.

The Capital Jury Project (CJP) studied jurors' understanding of the death penalty process (Bowers 1996). The CJP found that jurors did not keep the guilt and punishment phase discussions separated, with almost two-thirds of respondents acknowledging that discussions regarding punishment took place during the deliberations for guilt or innocence. In fact, the CJP found that 40% had discussed recommending a death sentence when determining the guilt of the defendant (Bowers 1996). The group also reported that 40% of jurors thought that a death sentence was mandatory if they considered the crime heinous, vile, or depraved (Bowers 1996). Finally, the majority of more than 800 jurors in 11 states in the sample substantially underestimated the amount of time a defendant would serve in prison if given a life sentence (Bowers 1996). This led them to recommend the death penalty more often since they did not believe that the defendant would spend the rest of his/her life in prison.[39]

The evidence on jury selection and of jurors' attitudes seems to demonstrate that the capital punishment system is skewed against the defendant and predisposes toward guilt. The exclusion of some members of society from capital juries is in conflict with the right to a jury of one's peers (Dieter 2005; Fleury-Steiner 2004). This has led to the development of more conservative juries, which in turn has resulted in more death sentences (Foley 2003). Those punishments are often highlighted by politicians as reasons for continuing with the use of

---

[39] The sample for this study seems to be rather unique. Members of the CJP interviewed four randomly selected jurors from each of 20-30 capital juries in 14 participating states. These subjects were interviewed for three to four hours about their decision making process during the capital trial that they served as a juror on. Due to the large sample size and the subjects' unique experience of having served on a capital jury, judges, prosecutors and defense attorneys could use this information to educate jurors as to the process of capital punishment and to dispel any misunderstandings of the process.

capital punishment, and although it is difficult to determine in some instances whether public opinion brings changes in politics or vice versa, it is undeniable that the two are closely related on the issue of capital punishment in the United States.

PROFESSIONAL ORGANIZATIONS AND THE DEATH PENALTY

In addition to states and the U.S. Supreme Court, many professional groups have weighed in on the issue of capital punishment. The American Bar Association (ABA), the American Medical Association (AMA), the American Nurses Association, the American College of Physicians, the American Public Health Association, the National Association of Emergency Medical Technicians, the American Society of Anesthesiologists and the Society of Correctional Physicians have either called for a moratorium on capital punishment in the United States and/or incorporated statements within their ethical policies that forbid their members from taking part in a legal execution.

One of the most vocal professional organizations involved in the debate is the American Bar Association (ABA). In recent years, the ABA has called for a moratorium on all executions until death penalty statutes can be written to resolve a myriad of problems currently plaguing the criminal justice system: "Today, administration of the death penalty, far from being fair and consistent, is instead a haphazard maze of unfair practices with no internal consistency" (ABA 2001:68).

In 2001, the ABA released a report on the increased number of moratoriums in the U.S. This report studied all the problems in the implementation of the death penalty and potential ways to solve those problems. The report outlines five areas that feature "serious deficiencies" – namely, the competency of State-appointed counsel in capital cases, the independence and thoroughness of post-conviction and *habeas corpus* review of capital cases, continuing racial discrimination in the exercise of discretion in capital cases, and imposition of the death penalty on the mentally retarded and on individuals who were under the age of eighteen at the time they committed capital offenses (ABA 2001).

A follow-up report by the ABA was completed in 2007 (ABA 2007). In its report, the ABA examined the death penalty systems in the eight states of Alabama, Arizona, Florida, Georgia, Indiana, Ohio,

Pennsylvania, and Tennessee. [40] For this sample, the researchers reviewed the policies and procedures of each state to determine whether the following issues were addressed: collection, preservation, and testing of DNA and other types of evidence; law enforcement identifications and interrogations; crime laboratories and medical examiner offices; prosecutorial professionalism; defense services; the direct appeal process; state post-conviction proceedings; clemency; jury instructions; judicial independence; the treatment of racial and ethnic minorities; and mental retardation and mental illness (ABA 2007). They reported that all the states in the study had deficiencies in at least one of those areas.

The American Medical Association (AMA) has long believed in the Hippocratic Oath of "do no harm" to patients. As capital punishment has become more medical in nature, the AMA has taken the stance that its members are prohibited from participating in the legal execution of a condemned prisoner (AMA 2003). The AMA has also endorsed a moratorium on the death penalty (AMA 2007). Consequently, doctors play only a small role, if any, in comforting the condemned in the final hours and pronouncing the executed inmate's death. [41]

In addition, the American Nurses Association (ANA), the American College of Physicians (ACP), the American Public Health Association (APHA), the National Association of Emergency Medical Technicians (NAEMT), the American Society of Anesthesiologists (ASA) and the Society of Correctional Physicians (SCP) are all

---

[40] "The ABA chose states based on a variety of factors, including the size of the state's death row, the number of anticipated problems in death penalty administration, and state bar enthusiasm and/or participation" (ABA 2007a:1).

[41] "There is a diverse range of lethal injection execution protocols and level of physician involvement. Just over one third of executing jurisdictions -- 13 states -- have formal execution protocols though recent court litigation suggests a lack of knowledge of the procedures by corrections staff and unreliable implementation of procedures in many cases. Twenty-seven states make reference to the medical role in the death penalty though again the laws and the roles expected of health personnel vary greatly" (Amnesty International 2007).

professional organizations that prohibit their members from taking part in a court-ordered execution. This begs the question: If no doctor, nurse, EMT, paramedic, board-certified anesthesiologist, and correctional physician is allowed to participate in executions, particularly those carried out by lethal injection, who would be qualified to insert the needles and prepare the drugs for the procedure?[42] In other words: "The providers in the system who see themselves as providing a valuable service to a population in great need, but who will not be party to execution, will leave the prison environment, thereby reducing the pool of available professionals" (Weisbuch, 1984:309).

From this brief historical and legal review, several issues are important to emphasize. First, the adoption or repeal of capital punishment legislation has a variety of influences, which include political, social and economic variables. In terms of political factors, some groups have been able to sway state legislators, such as the Quakers in Pennsylvania and the abolitionists in Michigan. These groups may not have been able to achieve their ultimate goal (i.e.,

---

[42] The Supreme Court recently heard arguments that questioned the constitutionality of lethal injection. The condemned argued that the lethal injection is cruel and unusual punishment (*Baze et al. v. Rees et al.*). A recent study on the effects of the drugs used in lethal injections has, in part, required the Supreme Court to revisit the constitutionality of this method of execution. Zimmers et al. (2007) studied the current method of lethal injection and reviewed execution data from North Carolina and California. They included interspecies dosage scaling and publications in clinical, laboratory and veterinary medicine in their analysis. The researchers concluded that the dosage of thiopental may not be sufficient to induce unconsciousness throughout the execution (Zimmers et al. 2007). They also determined that potassium chloride may not "reliably induce cardiac arrest" (Zimmers et al. 2007:0646). As a result, the condemned may only be paralyzed, but is being chemically asphyxiated (Zimmers et al. 2007). It is also important to mention that the drug cocktail used in lethal injection executions is prohibited when euthanizing animals (Alper 2006; Amnesty International 2007). Despite this research, the Court ruled that lethal injection is not cruel and unusual and executions have continued using this method.

complete abolition), but they were able to produce compromises, including the end of public executions and adoption of more humane methods for executions. The social factors include the tensions that Americans feel as a result of national and global events. As mentioned previously, although the early part of the twentieth century seemed to elicit an optimistic feeling in this country, entrance in World War I quickly changed that feeling to fear and tension. Finally, the economic factors seem to have strong influence on how Americans view crime and capital punishment. It is not a coincidence that the greatest number of executions occurred during the Great Depression. Mass unemployment led to not only greater levels of crime in the form of theft, but also in a greater fear of crime.[43]

Second, political, social, and economic factors appear to have a cyclical trend. As mentioned previously, the trends that Barrows noted at the turn of the twentieth century can be seen at the turn of the twenty-first century, with great influxes in between. The trends at both periods of time seem to be moving toward a more humane method of execution and abolishing the practice all together. Unfortunately, with the war in Iraq and the recent economic problems, this trend may again recede and could potentially result in additional numbers of executions as more people lose their jobs and experience having their home mortgages go into default. The poor classes may become an increasing threat to the upper and middle class, particularly as the gap between the rich and poor widens.

Finally, although the issues raised in the historical and legal overview do not expressly reveal the social inequality that is inherent within the American criminal justice system, it does provide for a context in which to analyze the current state of capital punishment.

---

[43] The recent trend to appeal death penalty statutes also has economic component. Since the recent recession hit the U.S. economy, states are attempting to find ways to make up for the deficits in their budgets. Most recently, Connecticut cited cost as the main reason for repealing its capital punishment statute. "Connecticut has been paying about $5 million a year to maintain its death penalty system, according to the state's Office of Fiscal Analysis, despite the fact it is rarely used. The only person the state has executed since 1960 is serial killer Michael Ross, who raped and murdered eight young women in the 1980s" (Bassett 2012).

Without this overview, it would be difficult to understand the present state of affairs when it comes to the death penalty. Also, given the various types of information presented, it is not difficult to understand why emotions tend to run high when discussing capital punishment in the United States. The next chapter will review previous studies on the death penalty in order to explain potential factors that may help predict whether a state adopts death penalty legislation and how it decides to implement it if provided for in state law.

CHAPTER 3

Literature Review

Research and commentary on capital punishment in the United States are thriving with publications rising in number. There are various recurring themes in published works that allow the groupings of articles across disciplines. This literature review will cover political, economic, racial/demographic, regional, and criminological factors in relation to the death penalty. It will also cover articles from various fields, such as economics, political science, sociology, criminal justice, and law.

POLITICS AND THE DEATH PENALTY

The democratic process in the U.S. has allowed citizens to weigh in on whether they are for or against the death penalty. Their opinions can be determined in public opinion polls, on juries, and within the political process. "Characteristics of the legislature (professionalism) affect the ideological orientation of state policy, but state opinion mediates the impact of the legislature on policy, at least in terms of the effect of the legislature's ideological orientation" (R. Jackson 1992:44). The combination of these forums has shown that historically the majority of Americans not only supports the death penalty, for murder in particular, but is willing to allow the elected officials to implement it as well.

As mentioned previously, the death penalty has become an increasingly political issue.[44] In fact, even though the majority of

---

[44] "Despite growing concerns about the fairness of the process and the risk of executing innocent people, most politicians have continued to support the death penalty. As one observer noted, 'Supporting the death penalty – saying so in public – is a way for an otherwise liberal and progressive-thinking man

45

executions are carried out by the state, and the President rarely deals with the issue of the death penalty, presidential candidates often debate the issue. Even judges, whose position it is to ensure that justice is served, are not immune from political pressures (Bright and Keenan 1995).[45] "As a practical matter, judges (particularly those elected from small rural areas) risk their jobs if they offend their constituents by changing the trial location" (Mullin 1980:142). Of the 38 states that had the death penalty in 1996, 32 elected, rather than appointed, their judges (Dieter 1996). Dieter (1996) also points out that a judge's stance on capital punishment, more than his/ qualifications for the job, affects the chances of election.

States have struggled with how to study and manage capital punishment in this politically charged era. In 1999, Governor Parris Glendening of Maryland funded a study to determine whether there is racial bias in the state's death penalty process (Maryland Citizens Against State Executions (MD CASE) 2007). Over the next three years, African American leaders pressured the Governor to impose a moratorium on the death penalty (MD CASE 2007). In 2002, Governor Glendening announced the moratorium, which he hoped would allow legislators and the public to review the study done by Dr. Raymond Paternoster (MD CASE 2007). However, acting on a campaign promise, newly elected Governor Robert Ehrlich lifted the state's ban on executions.[46] Capital punishment statutes in Maryland

---

or woman to flash tough-on-crime bona fides. Personally, they might think capital punishment is barbaric; they might believe in their hearts that no society that puts criminals to death can consider itself civilized. But they flash support for the ultimate penalty anyway' (Rodricks 2002)." (Acker, Bohm and Lanier 2003: 131).

[45] "A judge who faces election is more likely to sentence a defendant to death than a judge that heard the same evidence" (Bright and Keenan 1995:793). See also Uelman (1996) and Bright (1998) on the influence of politics on judges in death penalty cases.

[46] Maryland legislature established the Maryland Commission on the Death Penalty to provide recommendations for the future of the death penalty in Maryland. In arguing for abolition of the death penalty in Maryland, the Commission noted the following issues for coming to this recommendation:

were then repealed in 2013 by Governor Martin O'Malley. The Nebraska legislature also provided funds and a moratorium in order to study the death penalty process and trends in their state, overriding the governor's veto of the bill (Radelet and Borg 2000).

Despite those moratoria and commissioned studies, it is critical to take into account the overwhelming political tide that favors the death penalty. Since the re-enactment of capital punishment in 1976, many political candidates have run on a law and order stance.[47] Significantly, those who favor the death penalty are more likely to vote and elect these candidates. For example, Rankin (1979) found that those who voted for Nixon and Wallace, two candidates who promised to get tough on crime were more likely to support capital punishment (see also Garvey 2003). Rankin (1979) reviewed the correlation between the subjects' support for capital punishment and which candidate they voted for in the 1968 and 1972 presidential elections from data collected in the General Social Survey by the National Opinion Center between 1972 and 1976. Rankin's (1979) study indicated that the "politics of fear" succeeded in getting politicians elected. As Rankin points out crime rates increased dramatically in the 1960s, leading candidates to mention crime as a social problem of concern in their campaigns. Therefore, it is unclear whether the respondents were reacting to the rise in crime rates or the speeches of presidential candidates when it came to their opinion of the death penalty.[48]

Many researchers have found a strong correlation between support for capital punishment and conservatism (McCann 2008; Pardoe and Weidner 2004; Weidner and Frase 2003; Sorensen and Stemen 2002; Van Hiel and mervielde 2002; Eisenberg, Garvey, and Wells 2001; Huang et al. 1996; Eckhardt 1991; Nardulli et al. 1988; Wright,

---

racial and jurisdictional disparities, cost, the negative effect on victims' families, the risk of executing an innocent person, and the lack of deterrence.

[47] It is interesting to note that significant anti-death penalty movements in the 1840s, 1920s, and 1950s correlated with concerns of the liberal middle class for the treatment of prisoners (Hamm 2001). These periods of increased liberalism not only saw a decrease in support for the death penalty, but an increased desire to rehabilitate prisoners rather than just punish them.

[48] Please note that the unit of analysis for this study is individuals. This book, in contrast, will be examining states as the unit of analysis.

Erikson, and McIver 1985; Tyler and Weber 1982) or a closely related concept of fundamentalism (Paternoser, Brame and Bacon 2008; Young 1992). Huang et al. (1996) and Nardulli et al. (1988) based their analysis on individual court cases, while McCann (2008), Weidner and Frase, (2003) and Sorensen and Stemen (2002) examined states and counties.

Jacobs and Carmichael (2002) performed a panel analysis and a supplemental time-to-event analysis of death penalty adoption and implementation in select jurisdictions. After controlling for social disorganization, region, period, and violent crime, they found that conservativism and Republican strength increased the likelihood that capital punishment will be adopted by a jurisdiction.[49] They theorize that when taken with their finding, minority presence and economic inequality increase the likelihood that capital punishment will be adopted. According to Jacobs and Carmichael (2002), it appears that the death penalty is seen as a tool to control the "dangerous classes."

Jacobs and Kent (2007) performed a state-level time series study to explain public support for capital punishment and the number of executions using conflict theory as their analytical framework. While controlling for murders in death penalty states and Supreme Court decisions, these researchers found a strong correlation between public support for the death penalty and annual executions. Jacobs and Kent (2007) and Jacobs and Carmichael (2001) also found that Republican strength had a similar effect.[50]

Finally, Stucky, Heimer and Lang (2005:211) "argue[s] that the effect of partisan politics on punishment is conditional on how much electoral competition legislators face." These researchers noted that Republican presidential candidates used the crime issue to "appeal to working and lower middle-class whites" (Stucky, Heimer, and Lang 2005:213). The authors found that when positions are hotly contested in a jurisdiction and Republicans control the state legislature, there is

---

[49] Although there is discussion of conservativism and fundamentalism in these studies, I will only focus on the percentage of the state legislature that is Republican because previous research shows that Republicans tend to be more in favor of capital punishment than their Democratic counterparts.

[50] Interestingly, civil rights protests decreased support for the death penalty and the annual number of executions (Jacobs and Kent 2007).

an increase in imprisonment rates. In addition, larger states have higher imprisonment rates when political context is controlled for (Stucky, Heimer, and Lang 2005). Finally, their results seem to indicate "that welfare may serve as an alternative control institution in contemporary society" (Stucky, Heimer, and Lang 2005:231).

RACE AND THE DEATH PENALTY

America's system of slavery was brutal and continues to leave long lasting scars on our social institutions even today.[51] African-Americans have been overrepresented in American prisons, but underrepresented in political positions.[52] As a result, race remains a highly charged subject within criminal justice in general. This section will discuss research on the historical connection between the death penalty and the effect that the races of the victim and of the defendant have on capital punishment. While individual-level racial characteristics are not the focus of this book, the racism reflected in aggregate statistics showing

---

[51] "Arguments linking the death penalty to slavery and the social relations it established are strengthened by the strong relationships between race-specific measures of social well-being and death penalty intensity, particularly in light of the very weak relationship between percent Hispanic and death penalty intensity. In fact, with percent black so strongly linked to death penalty intensity (.677), the geography of race first established by slavery has a legacy as strong as the social relations rooted in this practice" (Lofquist 2001-2002:1535). See also Melusky and Pesto (2003) and Franck (2003).

[52] "The reality of the administration of criminal justice in the South is that a black defendant can still find himself facing a jury from which the overwhelming majority, if not all, of the prospective jurors of his race have been excluded. This is true even in counties that have black populations exceeding thirty or forty percent. Several factors contribute to this state of affairs. For one, the prosecutors overwhelmingly are white. Of the sixty-seven elected district attorneys in Alabama, one is black, and he is new to the job. None of Georgia's 159 counties has a black district attorney. There are also few black judges. It still is not uncommon for a black defendant to find herself the only minority group member in the entire courtroom" (Stevenson and Friedman 1994: 519).

the higher propensity of African-Americans to be affected by the death penalty varies by state and thus is of key interest here.

The lack of overall homogeneity in the American population has often led to discrimination, particularly in terms of systems of social control. Minorities that have been underrepresented in government and other decision-making bodies frequently become the target for initiatives that punish them for their race and/or ethnicity.[53] As a result, Nice (1992:1038) notes "race and capital punishment have been entangled for years." Nice (1992) notes that some studies have found that states with a higher percentage of African Americans are more likely to have death penalty provisions. However, after reviewing his citations, the studies Nice (1992) mentioned examined the influence that the races of the defendant and victim has on whether the death penalty is employed.

Many researchers have argued that the death penalty is implemented in a racist manner (Jacobs et al. 2007; Cortese 2006; Jacobs, Carmichael, and Kent 2005; McAllister 2003; Lofquist 2001-2002; Tabak 1999; Baldus et al. 1998; Dieter 1998; Stevenson and Fredman 1994; Galliher at al 1992; United States General Accounting Office 1990; Tushnet 1989; Kennedy 1988; Hartung 1952). In his analysis of capital punishment trends in the U.S., Hartung (1952) found that African Americans were overrepresented by 550% in execution numbers between 1930 and 1950. Particularly striking is the fact that only African American men were executed for the charge of rape during the period covered by Hartung's study (1930-1950).[54] After reviewing the historical data related to death penalty cases from the early part of the twentieth century, Galliher et al. (1992:541) found that "states with the highest concentrations of non-white citizens ha[d] used

---

[53] In a review of the demographic composition of district attorneys across the U.S., the Cornell Law Review found that only 1% of District Attorneys are African American, even though African Americans comprise 13% of the American population (Dieter 1998). "Whites, who as judges, prosecutors and jurors dominate the death sentencing process, cannot help feeling more indignation upon learning that a white (like them) has been killed than they do when there is a black victim" (Lempert 1983:1113).

[54] "Since 1930, nearly 90 percent of those executed for the crime of rape in the U.S. were Blacks" (Cortese 2006:4).

the death penalty most frequently." Dieter (1998) argues that when the defendant is African American, race is used as an aggravating factor in Philadelphia. African Americans were 3.9 times more likely to receive a death sentence than other defendants (Dieter 1998).

In addition, Cortese (2006) found that although African Americans make up 12.3% of the U.S. population, roughly 33% of those who were executed in 2004 were black. In addition, African Americans are disproportionately represented as both killers and victims, roughly 50% (Cortese 2006).

In recent studies, the race of the victim is also found to be a significant factor in predicting whether a defendant will receive the death penalty (Fleury-Steiner, Dunn and Fleury-Steiner 2009; Phillips 2008; Coyne and Entzeroth 2006; Millemann and Alexander 2006; Cortese 2006; Dow 2005; Haney 2005; Paternoster et al. 2003; Dow and Dow 2002; Unah and Boger 2001; Radelet and Borg 2000; Schaefer, Hennessy and Ponterotto 2000; Bobo and Smith 1998; Frierson et al. 1998; Radelet and Bedau 1998; Sarat 1998; Dieter 1997; Nice 1992; Baldus, Woodworth, and Pulaski 1990; United States General Accounting Office 1990; Jacoby and Paternoster 1982). Radelet and Bedau (1998) and Radelet and Borg (2000) found that defendants who were convicted of killing whites were 3 to 4 times more likely to receive a death sentence than those who were convicted of killing blacks. The General Accounting Office found a similar finding in its review of Georgia's implementation of the death penalty (Dieter 1997). Dieter (1997) notes that the findings of manifest racial discrimination are similar in other states. "In Illinois, the multiplier is 4, in Oklahoma it is 4.3, in North Carolina 4.4, and in Mississippi it is 5.5" (Dieter 1997).

Like Paternoster (2003), Cortese (2006) found that blacks who murdered whites were far more likely to be prosecuted in a capital case than any other victim/defendant race combination; moreover, blacks who kill blacks have the least chance of being capitally prosecuted. "The racial bias in the application of the death penalty is an indication of the extent to which social inequality affects the implementation of legal discretion" (Cortese 2006:19).

Phillips (2008:1) examined the impact that race had "on the District Attorney's (DA) decision to pursue a death trial and the jury's decision to impose a death sentence against adult defendants indicted for capital murder in Harris County (Houston), Texas from 1992 to 1999."[55] After controlling for defendants' characteristics[56], victim social characteristics[57] and legal dimensions of the case[58], Phillips (2008) found that the District Attorney pursued a death sentence for 30% of white victims, 26% of Hispanic victims, and 23% of African American victims. Similarly, after controlling for 36 different factors[59], Unah and Boger (2001) found that although the overall death-sentencing rate in North Carolina was low (2.8%), the white-victim cases had a rate almost twice as high as the non-white victim cases.

---

[55] Harris County sends more people to death row than any other county in the U.S.

[56] Sex, age, whether the defendant had a prior violent conviction, whether the defendant had a prior non-violent conviction, and the defendant's form of legal counsel.

[57] Sex, whether the victim was vulnerable due to age, and whether the victim had a prior violent or non-violent conviction

[58] Heinousness of the crime, whether multiple defendants were indicted, the form of capital murder, and the method of murder.

[59] Races of defendant and the victim, ages of the defendant and the victim, motive (hate, money, rage), multiple victims, sex of the victim, percent of the white population in the county, nonstatutory mitigating factors, nonstatutory aggravating circumstance of victim, defendant and victim are family members/intimates, prior homicide conviction record, murder method (poisoning, lying in wait, imprisonment, torture, starvation), willful, deliberate, and premeditated killing, felony murder, time from trial to district attorney's next reelection, District attorney's party affiliation statutory aggravating factors (felony committed by a lawfully incarcerated person, defendant previously convicted of another capital felony, previously convicted of violent felony, capital felony to avoid arrest, contemporary felony homicide, pecuniary gain, killing of law enforcement/judicial officer/fireman, heinous, atrocious, or cruel, great risk of death to more than one person, violence against another victim), and statutory mitigating factors (no prior history of criminal activity, under the influence of emotional disturbance, accomplice to felony committed by another person, under domination of another person, capacity to appreciate criminality impaired, consideration of defendant's at time of homicide, aided in apprehension of another capital felon).

These studies tend to be anecdotal in nature, but other studies seem to support the conclusions that those researchers have reached.[60]

Finally, Jacobs and Carmichael (2002) reviewed state-level data from 1970, 1980 and 1990 to explain the absence or presence of death penalty legislation in U.S states in 1971, 1981, and 1991. "After controlling for social disorganization, region, period, and violent crime, panel analyses suggest that minority presence and economic inequality enhance the likelihood of a legal death penalty" (Jacobs and Carmichael 2002:109). These researchers argue that the results support a political explanation of the differences among the states when it comes to capital punishment (Jacobs and Carmichael 2002). They theorize that when a population feels threatened, in this case by minorities because of their presence but also because of economic inequality in the area, its members will vote for those officials that address these concerns through punitive policies.

Despite the numerous studies that have been completed to examine the effect of race on the death penalty, it is important to mention that there are problems with the generalizability of the results. However, as Phillips (2008:24) points out, the research "combine[s] to form a composite picture" and that "the current research adds an important pixel."

CRIME RATES AND THE DEATH PENALTY

One of the leading arguments for the death penalty is based on issues related to crime. In particular, death penalty supporters tend to believe that capital punishment serves as a deterrent to murder, while opponents argue that the death penalty has the opposite effect (Clement 2002; Kronenwetter 2001). In addition, some studies theorize that crime rates, homicide and violent crime rates in particular, are used to instill fear in the public, impelling the adoption and the implementation of the death penalty.

The death penalty is meant not only to deter crime, but to punish criminals as well. Increases in crime, particularly violent crime, allow

---

[60] Although these studies focus on individuals, it is important to note that this research may reflect a systemic issue in the criminal justice system and state-level variation in executions.

for politicians to suggest adoption and implementation of a death penalty statute and for expanding the number of crimes that can constitutionally be punished with death. Archer et al. (1983) noted that the increased support for the death penalty in the late 1970s and early 1980s was the result of the increase in crime. Rankin (1979) found that respondents were more willing to employ harsh punishments if they were concerned about crime. In fact, he found that there was "[a] rather strong, positive, nonlinear relation between support for capital punishment and the violent crime rate" (Rankin 1979:207). This fact suggests that, although the death penalty does not deter crime, Americans are nonetheless more likely to favor harsh punishments if they feel that crime is a problem. By contrast, Tyler and Weber (1982) argue that the fear or concern over crime is not the reason citizens support capital punishment. Their study finds that people maintain their belief in the death penalty as a result of their basic political and social values (Tyler and Weber 1982). Therefore, even if crime rates were low, there would be a part of the population that would unequivocally support capital punishment.[61]

These studies show that no matter how questionable the deterrent effect of capital punishment on crime is, Americans nonetheless support the death penalty. Consequently, this support can arguably be either the result of a general fear in crime or the belief that if a person kills he/she should also be killed (retributive/"an eye for an eye" argument). Therefore, it is my contention that an increase in homicide rates should result in an increased likelihood that the state would adopt the death penalty.

Innocence

One of the most important issues plaguing death penalty policy in the U.S. is the potential for a wrongful conviction. As Radelet and Bedau

---

[61] It is important to note that these researchers are reviewing individual-level data, while this study focuses on states as the unit of analysis. However, this information is important in showing that (1) individuals can have an effect on policy adoption and implementation and (2) the adoption and implementation of a morality policy such as capital punishment is extremely complex and needs to be contextualized.

(1998) make clear, the criminal justice system is not proficient or accurate in determining who is guilty and who is innocent, let alone in fairly and consistently deciding who deserves life imprisonment and who deserves death.[62] The current record reflects this problem. From 1973 until 1992, sixty-eight inmates were released as a result of reasonable doubt regarding their guilt (Radelet and Bedau 1998). Since 1992, this number has more than doubled when Glenn Ford's exoneration in Louisiana brought the total number of people freed from death row to 144 (DPIC 2014c).

Dieter (1997) argues that the increase in exonerations is the result of two principal factors. First, the U.S. has increased its use of the death penalty convictions since its reinstitution in 1976, though this trend seems to be starting to decline. As a result, the overall number of death penalty cases has increased, which increases the odds (and number) of people who could be wrongly convicted and condemned. Second, capital punishment has become a political tool in campaigns for many elected officials, including prosecutors and trial court judges (Dieter 1997). In this case, it is more important to have many capital convictions, even if having fewer capital convictions reduces the risk of error. A lower number of capital convictions can be used against potential candidates as proof that they are not tough on crime.

It is important to note that few of those exonerations were the result of the appeals process; most were the product of work done by journalists and expert lawyers in addition to updated scientific tests (Dieter 1997). The use of DNA analysis and investigative techniques by journalism students, journalists, lawyers and law school students have played an increasingly important role in freeing innocent people from death row. Most death row inmates are indigent, which greatly reduces their chances of having the funds to bring their cases to public view. In addition, capital cases are expensive and complex, thus leaving few resources to fully investigate every claim of innocence.

Despite this fact, the appeals process has come under attack over the last ten years, prompting state and federal legislatures to block or limit access to both federal and state courts by imposing time

---

[62] Greenberg (1986:1672) found that between January 1, 1982 and October 1, 1985, "about forty-five percent of capital judgments which were reviewed during this period were set aside by one court or another."

restrictions and reducing the grounds for an appeal. The time between conviction and execution has been reduced to the point that there is an increased risk that more innocent people will be executed (Dieter 1997). According to Dieter (1997), prior to new legislation imposing restrictions on appeals, the average exonerated death row inmate spent eight years on death row. For forty-eight of the cases that he reviewed, it took an average of six and a half years to obtain a release based on innocence (Dieter 1997). In twenty-one more cases, the average time between conviction and release was approximately seven years (Dieter 1997). However, if the speed of the execution process were increased, so as to only provide four or five years between conviction and execution, many of those mistakes would not be discovered (Dieter 1997).

This problem is only exacerbated by the fact that it has become extremely difficult politically for governors and parole boards to commute death sentences. Commutations of death sentences have been used against incumbents during re-election campaigns to demonstrate the incumbents' lax treatment of crime. According to Radelet and Bedau (1998), only 29 death sentences were commuted between 1973 and 1992; nine of those were the result of evidence that put into question the guilt of the defendants (Radelet and Bedau 1998).

Finally, while some states have attempted to limit access to courts in the appeals process, other states have started to review their death penalty process. One of the most noteworthy of those is the state of Illinois. Prior to leaving office, Republican Governor George Ryan recognized that his state's death penalty policy was fraught with problems. He cited the fact that twelve people had been executed since 1976, while thirteen condemned prisoners were released based on serious questions regarding their guilt (Radelet and Borg 2000). Governor Ryan imposed a moratorium on Illinois' death penalty so that a study could be completed. He also pardoned four death row prisoners, and reduced the sentences of the rest of Illinois condemned prisoners either to life imprisonment or to prison terms of 40 years (DPIC 2007b).

These recent exonerations and commutations have changed the way some Americans view capital punishment. Unnever and Cullen (2005) found that 75% of Americans believed that an innocent person had been executed within the last five years and that this belief is held more by African Americans than whites. "In addition, our analyses revealed that believing an innocent person had been executed had a stronger association with altering African American than white support for the death penalty" (Unnever and Cullen 2005:3).[63] In light of these observations, I will examine whether exonerations are associated with the death penalty and the number of executions in a state.

Previous Studies on Differences of States' Capital Punishment Policies

As mentioned previously, researchers often study the region to determine trends in capital punishment legislation. Despite similarities between states within a region, not all states within a region are the same. Therefore, some researchers study factors within individual states to analyze differences in death penalty statutes or in number of state executions.

Researchers who study states and the death penalty take two distinct paths; some compare states with the death penalty against those without the death penalty; others provide studies on specific states. Although some have argued that the U.S. Supreme Court will provide the reason for the abolition of the death penalty, many still argue that it will be the responsibility of the states to make the determination of whether capital punishment has a place in the U.S. (Hochkammer 1969). Gerstein (1960) reveals that many states abolished the death penalty, but reenacted it when the policy makers and the public felt it would serve as a deterrent. Many prosecutors argue that "the retention of capital punishment is the State's right of self-defense" (Gerstein 1960:255). Also, the Supreme Court will review all state death penalty statutes to determine the excessiveness of a penalty (Fleming 1999). Therefore, an examination of state policies is vital to determine what trends emerge in America's use of the death penalty.

Galliher and Galliher (2001) point out that following the *Furman* decision, states with a tradition of executions and states that were part of the Confederacy were the first to implement new death penalty statutes. Their research also revealed that the death penalty is only enacted when

---

[63] Recently, the Columbia Human Rights Law Review published the study, "Did Texas Execute an Innocent Man?" Leibman et al. make the case that Carlos DeLuna was an innocent man executed by the state of Texas in 1989.

the governor promises to veto all capital punishment statutes (Galliher and Galliher 2001). Specifically studying the 19-year death penalty debate in New York State's legislature, Galliher and Galliher (2001) found that when the governor publicly expresses this kind of opposition, both houses of the state legislature seem to cooperate more in order to gain sufficient support to get a death penalty statute adopted.

In studies that compare states, it is important to examine the states that are being compared and the reasoning behind the comparisons made (Bailey 1974; Zeisel 1976). Bailey (1974) takes exception to these comparisons on the basis of scientific inquiry. He points out that this type of evaluation is faulty because no two states are exactly alike (Bailey 1974). The differences in statutes are not just the result of the state, but the "etiological factors – population composition, social structure and culture patterns" (Bailey 1974:416).

Norrander (2000) found that there was no correlation between public opinion and the existence of capital punishment in the Southern states in either 1936 or in the 1990s. However, she did find that in states with the death penalty, public opinion polls showed an increase of 7% in those favoring capital punishment over states that did not have the death penalty (Norrander 2000). She also noted greater support for capital punishment in states with a more urban population, while states with more African Americans and Catholics had lower levels of support for this policy (Norrander 2000). Finally, states with a history of executions were more likely to have the death penalty (Norrander 2000). As a result, each state's data must be examined to account for the factors that may predict whether a state retains or abolishes the death penalty.

Galliher and Galliher (2001) compared the homicide rates of New York in 1965 and 1991. They note that in 1991 murder rates were decreasing throughout the United States, and that New York was following this trend. Between 1976 and 1995, New York did not have a death penalty statute on the books. However, in 1995 when Governor George Pataki reinstated capital punishment homicide rates had decreased by 40% since 1990, "but they were still 86% higher than in 1965" (Galliher and Galliher 2001:316). Consequently, Governor Pataki was able to argue for the need of capital punishment using homicide rates, while failing to mention the pertinent fact that homicides were actually decreasing in the years leading up to the reinstatement of the death penalty.

Michigan is often referred to in the literature when it comes to abolition. Since becoming a state, Michigan never had a death penalty statute. According to David (2006), two events led to this decision. First, an innocent man (Patrick Fitzpatrick) was hanged for a rape and murder that he did not commit. Second, a public execution that started out as jubilant quickly became somber at the moment the condemned was hanged, thereby leaving the onlookers confused and concerned over their lack of humanity. As a result, Michigan does not respond to its high homicide rates with passage of a death penalty statute despite the fact that a majority of its citizens' support it (Schuessler 1952; Zeisel 1976).

Kansas is another state that is often studied. As mentioned previously, Kansas often had the death penalty, but it was largely inactive (Galliher and Galliher 1997). Schuessler (1952) found that although the homicide rate was high in Kansas between 1931 and 1935, which led to the reenactment of capital punishment in 1935, this trend was shared by its neighbor states. Galliher and Galliher (1997) reviewed the potential results and costs of Kansas implementing a newly designed death penalty statute. These researchers found that since the statute was narrow in the number and types of crimes that would result in a death sentence, there would only be between two and five cases annually (Galliher and Galliher 1997). They also noted that this was in line with the state's historical ambivalence toward capital punishment (Galliher and Galliher 1997). This ambivalence is particularly striking when one takes into account that in Kansas the African American population is higher than most other abolitionist states. African Americans comprise roughly 6% of Kansas' population, while other abolitionist states are a little below 3% (Galliher and Galliher 1997).

Rogers (1993) examined the history of the death penalty in Massachusetts. He found that Robert Rantoul, Jr. led the original abolition movement (Rogers 1993). Rantoul became an ardent opponent of the death penalty after his friend was wrongly convicted and executed for the murder of a wealthy businessman (Rogers 1993). However, his fight to abolish the death penalty was lost after some high profile cases called the entire criminal justice system into question. Questionable defense tactics in a few highly publicized capital cases caused the citizens of Massachusetts to support the death penalty. Abolitionism would not be taken up again for another hundred years, but this time it was met with success (Rogers 1993).

Bailey (1974) found that 67% of death penalty states had higher homicide rates than their abolitionist neighbors. Comparatively, only 20% of the abolitionist states had a higher homicide rate than their neighbors who had capital punishment (Bailey 1974). Only 13% of the comparisons had the same rate for both types of states (Bailey 1974). Although Bailey (1974) compared neighboring states, it is important to reiterate the fact that these states are not exactly alike. Therefore, the comparison on the basis of the presence or absence of death penalty statutes and proximity does not fully explain the homicide rates; other societal factors clearly must be considered.

Galliher and Galliher (1997) mention that the racial composition of the population is a predictive factor in states with the death penalty. Texas, Florida, Virginia, Louisiana, and Georgia were some of the first states to re-write their death penalty statutes after *Furman* (Galliher and Galliher 1997). These states carried out sixty-seven percent of the country's executions between 1976 and 1997 (Galliher and Galliher 1997). Interestingly, the average percentage of these states' populations that are African American is around 21% (Galliher and Galliher 1997).

Another important factor when examining the use of the death penalty in America lies in the study of regional differences. Many researchers have attempted to explain the ideological and political differences between states. Johnson (1976) used discriminate analysis to classify states using Elazar's political culture theory. Using state-level religious data to create indices, Johnson (1976) divided states between three mutually exclusive political system characteristics – moralistic, individualistic, and traditionalistic.

States with the largest death row population are not necessarily the most active.[64] As Figure 3 shows, California, Florida and Texas have

---

[64] States and number of executions (in parenthesis) since 1976 (as of June 25, 2012): Texas (513); Virginia and Oklahoma (110 each); Florida (85); Missouri (73); Alabama (56); Georgia and Ohio (53 each); North Carolina and South Carolina (43 each); Arizona (36); Louisiana (28), Arkansas (27); Mississippi (21); Indiana (20); Delaware (16); California (13); Illinois (12); Utah (7); Tennessee (6); Maryland and Washington (5 each); Idaho, Kentucky, Montana, Nebraska, Pennsylvania and South Dakota (3 each); Oregon (2); Colorado, Connecticut, New Mexico, and Wyoming (1 each) (Death Penalty Information Center 2014a).

the three largest death row populations in the country (DPIC 2012a). However, Texas and Virginia have the most active execution chambers in the United States, performing 450 executions since 1976 (DPIC 2012b). In fact, when George W. Bush was Governor of Texas, he signed off on 152 executions between 1995 and 2000 (Cook 2007).

Figure 3: Death Row Inmates by State as of January 1, 2013 (Death Penalty Information Center 2014c).[65]

State	# of Inmates	State	# of Inmates	State	# of Inmates
California	733	Oklahoma	57	Virginia	10
Florida	412	S. Carolina	50	Kansas	10
Texas	292	Missouri	48	Utah	9
Penn.	197	Mississippi	47	Washington	9
Alabama	197	Arkansas	38	U.S. Military	5
N. Carolina	160	Oregon	37	Maryland***	5
Ohio	145	Kentucky	34	Colorado	4
Arizona	125	Delaware	18	South Dakota	3
Georgia	95	Idaho	13	Montana	2
Louisiana	88	Indiana	12	New Mexico*	2
Tennessee	81	Nebraska	11	Wyoming	1
Nevada	80	Connecticut**	11	New Hampshire	1

[65] Source: Death Row Population Figures from NAACP Legal Defense and Education Fund, Inc. "Death Row Today" (July 1, 2013)
*New Mexico abolished the death penalty in March 2009, but law was not made retroactive so 2 remain on death row.
**Connecticut abolished the death penalty in April 2012 but law was not made retroactive so 11 remain on death row.
*** Maryland abolished the death penalty in May 2013 but law was not made retroactive so 5 remain on death row.

It is particularly interesting to examine where executions occur in terms of region. Amnesty International (2008) argues that there is a geographic arbitrariness when it comes to capital punishment in the U.S. As shown in Figure 4, the South accounts for the majority of executions since 1976: "Since the U.S. Supreme Court reinstated the death penalty in 1976, 80% of all executions have taken place in the South. The Northeast accounts for less than 2% of executions" (Amnesty International 2008:5). Lofquist (2001-2002) found that the use of the death penalty was strongly correlated with the history of slavery, whether the state was Union or Confederate, the number of lynchings from 1882 to 1968, and executions from 1930 to 1967. Of particular interest is the fact that Texas has carried out more executions post-*Furman* than any other state. Dieter (1994b) points out that in 1993 Texas was responsible for more than three times as many executions as any other state. As Garvey (2003) notes, the discrepancies between states is interesting, considering the increasing role the Supreme Court has played in developing the standards by which states may implement the death penalty. "The South has always led the nation in capital punishment, but the geographic disparities have grown over time. From the beginning of U.S. history until World War II, just less than 60 percent of all executions were in the South, with 22 percent in the Northeast, and 11 and 9 percent, respectively, in the Midwest and West. The percentage of executions in the northeastern states declined from 22 to 13 to 2 percent in successive periods, whereas that in the South increased from 59 to 61 to 80 percent" (Baumgartner, DeBoef and Boydstun 2008: 32-33). According to Jackson, Jackson, and Shapiro (2001), a murderer in the South is three times more likely to be sentenced to death than anywhere else in the U.S.

These regional and state studies reflect the need to account for factors in all 50 states instead of attempting to compare a few states in the hope of creating results that can be generalized to the rest of the country. Consequently, the current study will use measurements from all 50 states and control for regional effects.

Figure 4: Executions by Region since 1976 (Death Penalty Information Center 2014d).

Executions by Region	
Region	Total
South	1122
Midwest	164
West	84
Northeast	4
Texas & Virginia Alone	623

LITERATURE REVIEW SUMMARY

The literature review has highlighted some of the potential social, economic, and political factors that are relevant to the implementation of the death penalty. It appears that Republican-led states are more likely to implement the death penalty. In addition, race plays an important role in the implementation of the death penalty, particularly when using the percentage of the population that is African American as a measure. Exonerations and education also appear to have some effect on Americans' view of the death penalty and may affect the number of executions. In addition, homicide rates are not surprisingly highly correlated to the implementation of a death penalty statute, and thus need to be controlled in a model examining executions. Similarly, hate crimes may affect death penalty adoption and implementation. Finally, regional variations in execution rates need to be taken into account.

CHAPTER 4

Theoretical Framework

Several social scientists from a wide range of disciplines have attempted to explain state differences when it comes to policies; others have tried to find methods of lumping states into categories based on specific models and particular criteria. This section first provides an explanation of the theories that cover morality policies; second, it sets forth an overview of how policies are diffused; third, it presents a description of Kingdon's Garbage Can model; fourth, it develops an outline of some social control theories; and finally, the chapter concludes with a summary of the integrated policy framework that is employed in this study.

STATE MODELS

There are many models that attempt to explain the differences in policies between states. According to scholar Daniel Elazar, states with a moralistic political culture are governed by key actors who generally believe that government should be established to promote the public good. Politics are maximally participatory by intent and citizens' participation in these states is seen as inherently beneficial (Jackson 1992). In addition, these states tend to be more liberal or progressive in their social and economic policies (Jackson 1992). States in New England, in the Upper Midwest, and in the Northwest have been identified as moralistic (Gray, Hanson, and Jacob 1999). "Although a moralistic culture may not heighten the translation of citizen preferences into policy, it does appear that the political leaders in moralistic states operate within distinctive environments that enable them to promulgate liberal policies" (Jackson 1992: 44).

In contrast, states that tend to be individualistic in political culture are governed by key actors who generally believe that government should be limited in scope and purpose, emphasizing maintenance of the marketplace and associated activities (Gray, Hanson, and Jacob 1999). Elected officials in these states tend to pursue office in order to advance themselves and their interests professionally; unlike public officials in moralistic states they do not direct their work toward the common good directly, but rather feel that the simultaneous pursuit of self-interest will result in the collective achievement of the public good (Gray, Hanson, and Jacob 1999). According to Jackson (1992:38), individualistic states tend to experience "heightened translation of citizen preferences into policy." The Mid-Atlantic States, New York, Pennsylvania, the lower Mid-west, Missouri and the Western states have been identified as individualistic (Gray, Hanson, and Jacob 1999). "Thus, other things being equal, policy is far more responsive to public demands in those states with an individualistic political culture" (Jackson 1992: 42).

States that have been identified as traditionalist, i.e., in political culture, have fewer people participating in politics, and tend to view the role of government as maintaining the *status quo* (Gray, Hanson, and Jacob 1999). In these states, citizens are not expected to participate in politics to any great extent, leaving public policy matters to "those in the know" and enjoying "connections and social status" not commonly shared. There is no strong connection between the government and its citizens in this political culture setting (Jackson 1992). Southern states have been identified as being predominantly traditionalistic in their political culture. According to Jackson (1992: 45), "traditionalistic states oppose both new programs and governmental interventions into the economic and social life of the community, unless these interventions and programs are necessary to maintain the existing power structure."

According to Gray, Hanson, and Jacob (1999), state policy differences are the result of five overarching factors – people, place, economic context, political context, and states' ability to govern. The authors further argue that people – specifically, population size, population growth, population density, population composition, age, poverty, immigrants, and minorities – affect the adoption and implementation of policies. Each of these areas has an influence on how a population perceives their surroundings and what social problems exist in their communities.

The "place" of state, which includes land, historical political conflicts, location and climate, and natural resources, also impacts policies. Gray, Hanson, and Jacob (1999) argue that politicians in smaller states have an easier time campaigning than those in larger states. Also, smaller states are in less of a need of policies (and money) for the building and maintenance of roads. The authors point out that the tug of war over land between Western states and the Federal Government affected how the populations in those states view land rights. The location and climate can either help or hinder the attraction of businesses to the states. States with less hospitable weather, or those not located close to railways or other means of transportation, may adopt policies that would encourage businesses to locate there despite these detriments by offering incentives, such as tax breaks. Finally, natural resources, which also feed into the economic context of the state, can affect policies, particularly when it comes to soil, water, mineral and energy resources.

The economic context of the state includes the state economic activities and state personal income. State economic activities include what sector the majority of the jobs in the state reside, e.g., finance, insurance, real estate, services, manufacturing, or government, whereas the state income may constrain state programs (Gray, Hanson, and Jacob 1999).

The political context, according to Gray, Hanson, and Jacob (1999) includes historical differences, contemporary differences and national forces, including political and economic forces.[66] The racial and ethnic diversity, public opinion, and state political organizations all are highlighted as playing a role in the adoption and implementation of policies.

Finally, the states' ability to govern has been outlined as the final reason for the presence of differences in the adoption and implementation of policies across states, according to Gray, Hanson, and Jacob (1999). This includes the growth and decline of economy in the states, the distribution and redistribution of resources in the state, the increased diversity of populations, and the tug-of-war over power

---

[66] See above for discussion of Elazar's subcultures.

between states and the federal government (Gray, Hanson, and Jacob 1999).

MORALITY POLICIES

According to theorists, policies can fall into a wide range of categories, including but not limited to social, economic, urban, educational, and moral. "Morality policy raises questions that instigate debate over first principles, resulting in uncompromising clashes of values..." while non-morality based policies usually invoke discussion over economic issues that can be resolved through negotiation and compromise (Mooney and Lee 1995:600). According to Mooney and Lee (1995), morality policies allow for a greater number of people to be relatively knowledgeable about the subject and may want to voice their opinions.[67] "Debate is characterized by conflict over first principles, rather than conflict over how well a policy will achieve an agreed-on goal" (Mooney and Lee 1999a:82-83). The second characteristic of morality policies is that "these policies deal with the reallocation of strong symbols and values, people often pay attention to the debate and make their preferences known to policymakers" (Mooney and Lee 1999a:83).

Since the death penalty has been identified as a morality policy, a review of theories that attempt to explain why these policies are adopted and implemented in the first place is required. The first principle that seems very salient when it comes to the death penalty is the doctrine of double effect, which was first introduced by Saint Thomas Aquinas (McIntyre 2004). This doctrine states that actions that seem to be impermissible because of the serious harm that could result from them are justified when the side effect promotes a positive end (McIntyre 2004). Arguably, the death penalty might seem to be

---

[67] Morality policies are often designated as redistributive policies. "Since morality policy validates certain basic values and rejects others, it redistributes moral values just as surely as a progressive income tax scheme redistributes economic values" (Mooney and Lee 1999b:768). In addition, these policies tend to be simpler technically, since there are clear winners and clear losers (Mooney and Lee 1999b:768). In other words, there is no compromise.

justifiable if the act of executing a person will protect other members of society, either from the person who is being executed or by others who may commit murder if capital punishment were abolished. Michael Walzer has added another element to this principle; he argues "that agents minimize the foreseen harm even if this will involve accepting additional risk or foregoing some benefit" (McIntyre 2004). McIntyre (2004) provides the example of the hastening of the passing of a terminally ill patient to alleviate pain, even if there is the possibility that treatment or a cure will be developed in the near future.

Warren Quinn injects the idea of direct and indirect agency into this principle (McIntyre 2004). Direct agency involves intention and the ability to foresee possible effects, whereas indirect agency involves action taken as a result of someone else's action. For example, a person attempts to murder a person (intent) and devises a way to do so (foreseeable effects); this person is a direct agent in this scenario. The intended murder victim may attempt to fight back and unintentionally kill his attacker; this person is an indirect agent. However, according to McIntyre (2004) this interpretation violates "the victim's right not to be subordinated in this way" since indirect agency has been a disfavored kind of conduct.

According to the doctrine of double effect, even though society sees the untimely death of a human being as wrong, the population may allow the government to partake in the execution of convicted killers if the population deems that the public good is being addressed. Oftentimes, some will state that one execution can save a number of lives because that one killer has been permanently incapacitated. Others would use this principle to argue that if one execution prevents (or deters) another murder, then the public good has been served.

Another method for allowing for morality policies is the principle of utilitarianism. This theory was first developed by Jeremy Bentham, but was later expanded by John Stuart Mill and Mary Wollstonecraft, among others. According to Mill (1859), actions should be analyzed in a way that allows for the maximum amount of good for the maximum number of people. In other words, when determining whether a policy should be implemented, a review of the utility of the policy (i.e., the positive and negative consequences) should be completed. Arguably, the utility of capital punishment lies in the fact that society is being protected from a convicted murderer, and is thus justifiable in utilitarian terms. The permanent incapacitation of the condemned ensures that society will be safe from a person who threatened the population before. Although death may not be highly desirable, the safety of the citizenry justifies the extreme governmental action of taking a life.

On the opposite side of this argument lies negative utilitarianism. First expounded by Popper (1952), this theory states that actions should not be reviewed to maximize pleasure for the greatest number of people, but should instead analyze actions in an attempt to prevent the greatest amount of suffering. Under this line of argument, the execution of a person deemed to be dangerous minimizes the future risk that the person will hurt or kill another person. Therefore, when weighing the potential of future violence against the rights of the condemned, it may be argued that the consequences favor capital punishment.

Finally, when evaluating morality policy, some have argued for principlism to be employed in the analysis. First outlined in the Belmont Report and expanded by bioethicists Beauchamp and Childress (2001), principlism suggests that humane intententional actions should be reviewed on the basis of four moral principles – autonomy, beneficence, non-malfeasance, and justice.[68]

Unfortunately for proponents of capital punishment, principlism does not provide much justification for the continued use of the death penalty. Autonomy, also referred to as "respect for the person," would preclude governmental officials from partaking in executions, even if they argued that this principle refers to the respect of the victims. Although an execution may protect society from a given person, the beneficence principle requires that every person (offenders included) is treated with dignity and respect, a situation that is currently lacking in the implementation of the death penalty in the U.S.

---

[68] The Belmont Report holds that review of research involving human subjects should require a structured review that included respect for persons (autonomy), beneficence, and justice. Beauchamp and Childress (2001) included non-malfeasance in their *Principles of Biomedical Ethics*. Although the Belmont Report and Beauchamp and Childress (2001) specifically apply these principles to human subjects research, other researchers have applied them to the review of morality policy as well.

Non-malfeasance requires that an action cannot harm, which can be argued in two ways when it comes to the death penalty. First, the condemned is being harmed by living on death row for years before being executed, not to mention the pain and anguish his/her family must endure as a result. Second, as noted previously, some researchers argue that the death penalty results in a brutalization effect; that is, instead of deterring murders, it actually increases the likelihood of more murders in some situations.

Finally, justice requires a review of who is burdened by the action. "An injustice occurs when some benefit to which a person is entitled is denied without good reason or when some burden is imposed unduly" (The National Commission for the Protection of Human Subjects of Biomedical and Behavioral Research 1979). As mentioned previously, minorities and the poor tend to be overrepresented in the American justice system in general, and particularly among those selected for the ultimate punishment in particular.

Regardless of how policies will be reviewed, it is important to note how and why policies are adopted and the path they take to spread from community to community and from state to state. An examination of the diffusion of policy should explain why one region of the country adopts one form of a policy, while another might implement a completely different one, even if they are attempting to solve the same problem.

DIFFUSION OF POLICIES

Many researchers have argued that states adopt policies that have been adopted and successful in neighboring states (Mooney 2001; Stream 1999; Mooney and Lee 1995; Berry and Berry 1990; Lutz 1986; Light 1978; Walker 1969; Sutherland 1950; McVoy 1940; Davis 1930)

According to Mooney and Lee (1995:599), there are "three dimensions of the adoption process," regardless of whether the policies are morality policies or economically based policies. The first dimension is diffusion. This usually involves regional leaders adopting a policy and state neighbors within the same region adopting the same policy (Mooney and Lee 1995). The second dimension is policy reinvention. "Reinvention is the extent to which and the ways in which a policy is changed as it diffuses through the states" (Mooney and Lee

1995:608). Finally, adoption determinants, which may include "socioeconomic, political and public opinion characteristics," affect whether a policy is adopted in a given state (Mooney and Lee 1995:601).[69]

The adoption process relies on the "social learning model of decision-making" (Mooney and Lee 1999b:767). Mooney and Lee (1999b) argue that a new policy is first adopted by a few states. Other states then review the outcomes of the new policy before deciding whether to adopt the policy. "As time passes, a few more relatively adventurous states adopt the policy, and as its benefits become clear, more and more states adopt it with increasing frequency" (Mooney and Lee 1999b:767).

According to Meseguer (2005), there are two types of learning: rational and bounded. Rational learning involves the use of analytical capabilities (Meseguer 2005). Politicians comprehensively review the appropriate material related to a policy and make a decision based on that information. In contrast, bounded learning involves the use of that information and those data that are relatively close at hand to reach a decision on action at a moment in time when action is possible (Meseguer 2005). Meseguer (2005) notes that there are two main differences between learning and emulation. First, learning involves identifying a problem and finding a solution (Meseguer 2005). "Second, a solution is chosen on the basis of observed experience and a *better understanding* of which policies may lead to partiular outcomes" (Meseguer 2005:73, emphasis in original). On the other hand, emulation does not involve problem solving and is usually influenced by other motivations (Meseguer 2005). "Because governments emulate following certain trends, emulation becomes a symbolic act whereby politicians seek to enhance their status, credibility, or 'modernity'" (Meseguer 2005:79)."

Bennett and Howlett (1992) argue that there are three complex types of learning that affect the adoption of policy: Government, Lesson Drawing, and Social.

---

[69] Mooney and Lee (1995) applied these dimensions to explain the diffusion of abortion regulation reform, and found all three at work within the implementation and adoption of policies that address that issue.

Table 1: Three Types of Learning and Policy Change

LEARNING TYPE	WHO LEARNS	LEARNS WHAT	TO WHAT EFFECT
Government	State Officials	Process-Related Change	Organizational Learning
Lesson-Drawing	Policy Networks	Instruments	Program Change
Social	Policy Communities	Ideas	Paradigm Shift Learning

(Bennett and Howlett 1992:289).

As Table 1 above shows, there are many groups within the policy making process, but the lessons and effects of each are different. Additionally, Minstrom (1997) argues that policy entrepreneurs play an important part in the diffusion of public policies. Policy entrepreneurs network across states and "learn more about the details of policy innovations elsewhere" (Minstrom 1997:739-740). According to Minstrom (1997), this allows policy entrepreneurs to provide credible answers to questions regarding the new policy. Networking also allows them to make contacts with experts from other states in the event that outside parties are brought into the discussion over the ramifications of a new policy and to provide arguments for its adoption (Minstrom 1997). However, policy entrepreneurs are usually successful early in the process of diffusion (Mooney 2001). "With little information available other than that a neighbor has recently adopted it, an optimistic policy entrepreneur can spin this information to his or her advantage" (Mooney 2001:119).

It is important to note in this discussion of policy diffusion that "no two ideas diffuse in exactly the same way" (Walker 1969:896-897). A state usually needs to feel that their citizens will benefit in some way if a particular policy is adopted or that a policy fulfills a need that the state is deprived of being served (Walker 1969). In addition, Elkins and Simmons (2005) argue that using models that are close at hand constitutes a reason-based bias to the policy adoption process in many different areas of public policy.

Despite this fact, Mooney and Lee (1999b:778) note that "when the conflicts of first principle cannot be suppressed, social learning by political decision makers no longer drives the process." As a result, morality policies, such as capital punishment, are principally adopted at the behest of citizens. Elkins and Simmons (2005) argue that the adoption of a particular public policy often changes as a result of three primary factors: cultural norms, support groups, and competition. The form that capital punishment provisions will take, whether applied broadly or narrowly, will be determined by these three influences.

Although these constructs may explain state differences, further examination is required to explain who is being targeted and why they are being targeted. Stated a different way, it is important to analyze who is burdened with policies related to the death penalty.

DIFFUSION OF CAPITAL PUNISHMENT POLICIES

According to Mooney and Lee (1999a), there are five "dimensions" upon which death penalty reform spread. First, states began to limit the types of crimes that were punishable by death as early as 1794 (Mooney and Lee:1999a). Second, in 1834, states began passing legislation that required executions to be performed out of public view (Mooney and Lee: 1999a). Third, by the beginning of the twentieth century legislatures gave "judges and juries discretion in applying the death penalty to those convicted of first-degree murder" (Mooney and Lee 1999a:85). Fourth, executions were centralized.[70] Finally, humane methods of executions were adopted (Mooney and Lee 1999a).

Despite these early reforms, Mooney and Lee (1999a) found that states did not exhibit signs of social learning when it came to the adoption and comprehensiveness of their capital punishment legislation. In other words, death penalty legislation is adopted and implemented as a result of citizens' concerns rather than the result of learning from neighboring states. Mooney and Lee (1999b) also argue that the diffusion patterns of morality and nonmorality policies are very different. In order for a morality policy to diffuse similarly to another type of policy (ex. economic), particularly if it is an unpopular morality

---

[70] Prior to 1864, executions were performed in the jurisdiction that the crime took place.

policy, legislators (or policy entrepreneurs) must "de-moralize" the policy (Mooney and Lee 1999b). The characteristics that make it a morality policy must be neutralized so that it is no longer about what is viewed as right and wrong, but is instead viewed as a solution to a tractable problem.

TARGET POPULATIONS

Schneider and Ingram (1993) state that there are two overriding motivations for elected officials to develop public policies. First, they set their sights on re-election. Producing acceptable and politically popular policies enable them to argue the reasons they should be able to keep their present posts. The second reason is to solve or ameliorate a social problem (Schneider and Ingram 1993).

Every policy has rewards and burdens that are inflicted upon the population. Schneider and Ingram (1993:336) argue that negatively constructed groups bear a disproportionate burden because elected officials "need fear no electoral retaliation from the group itself and the general public approves of punishment for groups that it has constructed negatively." These authors outline four groups based on power (positive or negative) and social construction (positive or negative).[71] Those who have power and are viewed in a positive light by society are considered "advantaged" in Schneider and Ingram's model. This group includes the elderly, businessmen, veterans, and scientists. Those who have power and are viewed in a negative manner are considered "contenders." This group includes the rich, big unions, minorities, cultural elites, and the moral majority. Those who have no power, but have a positive construct are considered "dependents," a category which includes children, mothers, and the disabled. The final group, which contains people who have no power and are negatively constructed, is labeled "deviants." As the name conveys, these people include criminals, drug addicts and gangs, as well as communists and flag burners (figure can be found at Schneider and Ingram 1993:336).

---

[71] The concept of the social construction of target populations refers to: (1) the recognition of the shared characteristics that distinguish a target population as being socially meaningful; and, (2) the attribution either favorable or unfavorable images to these characteristics (Schneider and Ingram 1993).

Those who are negatively constructed and powerless are not only more likely to be burdened, but they are more likely to be incarcerated and executed than the advantaged populations (Schneider and Ingram 1993). According to Schneider and Ingram (1993), the deviants are portrayed as a problem and in need of punishment. To make matters more troubling yet for this group, political participation, whether it is voting or running for office, seems to be a moot point since "government belongs to someone else" (Schneider and Ingram 1993:342; see also Owen and Owen 2003). In fact, behaviors that are associated with the deviants are more likely to be criminalized (Schneider and Ingram use drug and alcohol abuse as an example); it is only when the behaviors are engaged in more widely by the advantaged that they become acceptable for political action (Schneider and Ingram 1993).

Within this model, the undue burden of capital punishment on minorities and the poor is explained. A lack of power and a negative social construction allows elected officials to justify increased punishment on groups that are commonly viewed as threatening. In areas where there is a higher proportion of minorities, middle- and working class whites might feel threatened and attempt to maintain their favorable social position by electing officials that speak to this fear (Jacobs and Carmichael 2002). In addition, difficult economic times may lead to a negative social construction of the chronically unemployed, which could lead in turn to policies that punish the unemployed more severely for trivial offences (Jacobs and Carmichael 2002). Jacobs and Carmichael (2002) and Chambliss and Seidman (1980) note that increased inequality leads to more coercive forms of punishment, including capital punishment, in an attempt to maintain the *status quo*. "Society used the death penalty not only to oppress minorities and protect the majority, but also as a repressive response to depression-era conditions of social dislocation and economic turmoil" (Galliher et al. 1992:576).

SOCIAL CONDITIONS – RACE, CLASS, AND SOCIAL DOMINANCE

As stated previously, race and class are recurring themes within the death penalty literature. Consequently, sociological theories outlining racial tensions, inequality, and the use of social control to maintain the *status quo* are necessary to explain the trend in the implementation of capital punishment in the U.S. "An execution is an intrinsically political act. Foucault (1977) views executions as rituals designed to enhance political power by reminding potential miscreants of the state's vast coercive resources" (Jacobs et al. 2007: 611).

According to Wacquant (2001a:82), stricter criminal justice policies have been applied to control groups that have fallen victim to what he refers to as an "era of employment insecurity." He argues that this era is characterized by a shift to service oriented jobs that do not have the same stability as blue collar, union jobs, a phenomenon that he states is present in France and the U.S. alike (Wacquant 2001a). The punitive criminal justice policy, according to Wacquant (2001a), is used in three ways. First, it is used as discipline for those who attempt to protest "the new, precarious service jobs" (Wacquant 2001a:82). Second, it removes "disruptive elements," essentially neutralizing them and their message of social discontent. (Wacquant 2001a:82). Finally, "it reaffirms the authority of the state in the limited domain that is henceforth assigned to it" (Wacquant 2001a:82; Wacquant 2001b:405).

Wacquant (1999) argues that the underlying justification for this increased repression "is in perfect harmony with neoliberal common sense on the economic and social front." According to the "neoliberal penality" argument, more prisons and police are needed to maintain the social order, even as they argue for less government "on the economic and social front[s]" (Wacquant 2003:198). In other words, criminal sentencing policy should follow the same logic as economic efficiency that markets have, and it is not the responsibility of society to assist or alleviate the problems of at risk populations, but rather the responsibility of individuals to survive and obey the social order (Wacquant 1999; 2001b). As a result, prisons and incarcerations are tools of social control during times of social insecurity and upheaval (Wacquant 2001b). According to Wacquant (2001b), these social problems are the direct result of "neo-liberal policies of economic deregulation and social-welfare retrenchment" (401). "The *invisible hand of the market and the invisible fist of the state combine* and complement each other to make lower classes accept desocialised wage labour and the social instability it brings in its wake" (Wacquant 2001b: 404; emphasis in original).

Parenti (1999) makes similar economic arguments to explain the increased incarceration rates in the United States. He contends that the first round of anti-crime initiatives occurred in the 1960s and was designed to combat counterinsurgency that many police departments did not know how to manage. There was also an increase in crime during the 1960s to which middle class Americans had not been accustomed, a situation which led to "a political opening for a change in the crime policy that ultimately increased the incarceration rate" (Western 2006:48). In addition, the riots and social upheaval of the 1960s paved the way to dramatic social changes in the U.S. that was "characterized by urban deindustrialization" (Western 2006:48-49). This wide scale deindustrialization in many U.S. cities and major metropolitan areas resulted in high unemployment and low wages, thus providing a justification for an increasingly punitive criminal justice system that would predictably concentrate enforcement actions on the most disadvantaged (Western 2006).

The second wave of "anti-crime repression" occurred in the early to mid-1980s as a reaction to the instability that resulted from "Reaganomic restructuring" (Parenti 1999:167). In order for the new business order to be successful, it became imperative to control and contain the poor (Parenti 1999). This is evidenced by the high incarceration rates of those that are considered to be part of the "dangerous class" – "poor African American, Latino, and Native American people, particularly men" (Parenti 1999:168). Finally, stereotypes of the underclass led middle class Americans to fear "the most potent anti-poor symbol" – "the young dark criminal, the untamed urban buck, running free threatening order, property, and (white) safety" (Parenti 1999:168).

Thus, a variety of researchers from various academic disciplines have concluded that race and class inequality account to a great extent for the dramatic increase in incarceration rates in the U.S. (Western 2006). According to Western (2006), class inequality contributed approximately 20 percent of this increase. Furthermore, Western (2006:36) argues that researchers have found a strong statistical link "between violent crime and economic racial inequality." In fact, homicide rates are highest in areas with high poverty and unemployment rates and high rates of divorce (Western 2006).

Although Wacquant, Parenti, and Western state that imprisonment is used to maintain social order in general, Mitchell and Sidanius (1995:592) argue that capital punishment is "an instrument of social hierarchy enforcement" with a particularsharp focus. According to Mitchell and Sidanius (1995:592) social dominance theory involves three factors that are utilized to maintain the social hierarchy: "behavioral asymmetry, individual discrimination, and ... institutional discrimination." This theory holds that dominant groups in society have greater social value than those of minority or subordinate groups and consciously endeavor to maintain that privileged position (Mitchell and Sidanius 1995).[72]

However, McCann (2008) argues that this symbolic threat is largely a unconscious phenomenon. Drawing on Judges' (1999) Terror Management Theory (TMT), McCann argues that capital cases involve the three elements of TMT. The first element is a "reminder of mortality" (McCann 2008:914). Clearly, a murder reminds us all that we are not immortal, but the premature death of a person cannot go unpunished. The second element requires "time to push awareness of it [the murder] to the fringes of consciousness" (McCann 2008:914). The mass media remind Americans daily that we live in a dangerous time by highlighting crimes, particularly recent murders. Finally, the public

---

[72] "The "undeserving poor" do pose a threat, but not to corporate and political elites. These disparate groups of unassimilated immigrants, welfare recipients, and criminals instead pose a symbolic threat to individuals who are serious stakeholders in the existing normative order. (In the context of the United States, commentators refer to this segment as "angry young White males" [Hogan, Chiricos, and Gertz 2005].) However, we do not assume that the normative order is one characterized by norms and values that are equally shared by all. Certainly, the persistence of the racial divide in support for the death penalty excludes this possibility. Instead, the data indicate that the normative order in Western-style democracies includes within it groups of individuals that harbor racial and ethnic animosities. The segments of the population that harbor racial and ethnic sentiments associate crime with the "undeserving poor." The end result of this typification process is that racists righteously believe that criminals and their kind deserve to be punished to the fullest extent of the law" (Unnever, Cullen, and Jonson 2008:85).

must have "an opportunity to indulge in punitive and often authoritarian aggression against an offending target person" (McCann 2008:914). This comes into play when an alleged murderer is put on trial by a jury of his/her peers and the prosecution argues for an extreme punishment for the crime. According to Judges (1999) and McCann (2008), Americans do not consciously defend themselves against this symbolic threat and capital punishment is not used "as a rational process in the service of retribution, deterrence, or incapacitation" (McCann 2008:914). Therefore, the threats that are being fought are not as coherent as some would argue, according to this theory.

The theories outlined thus far have elements similar to classical conflict theory, a theory used by Jacobs and Kent (2007) to explain the results of their study on capital punishment. According to Jacobs and Kent (2007:298), "[t]he racial and economic divisions emphasized in conflict theory and the mass protests that result help shape public and elite views about punishment" (Jacobs and Kent 2007:298). These researchers found that inequality was positively correlated with public support and executions, while civil right protests were negatively correlated with public support for the death penalty (Jacobs and Kent 2007). Arguably, this research could substantiate the Schneider and Ingram model based on positive and negative social constructions of groups in the political arena. Civil rights protests have the power to not only give power to those who historically have not had it, but it has the potential to provide populations previously viewed as deviants a substantially more positive social construction.

Additionally, these results may also provide evidence that the power-threat theory has some merit. Cortese (2006) argues that the increasing numbers of minorities have resulted in the white dominant group utilizing legal control to maintain the *status quo*, i.e. minorities in an economically and politically inferior position to whites. "Power-threat theory attributes racial prejudice and discrimination to competition for economic and political power" (Cortese 2006:11). This is an argument within the same realm as Wacquant, Parenti, and Western. According to Cortese (2006), imprisonment and executions are used to reduce the economic competition imposed by young African American men, thus affirming the power and privilege of the white majority.[73] This is an important part of policy implementation, since there are symbolic messages embedded in policies (Schneider and Ingram 1993). The embedded messages convey the social construction of different groups that are being targeted, and thus influence the policy agenda, but provide "the rationales that legitimate policy choices" (Schneider and Ingram 1993:334).

In addition to the messages instilled in policies, cultural transmission influences the social construction of groups (Cortese 2006). According to Cortese (2006), citizens will begin to believe that some groups are destined to be disproportionately imprisoned and condemned when they grow up in a society marred by persistent inequality. If minorities are overrepresented in lower paying jobs and are viewed as having a lower status, then other members of society will see their mistreatment and inequality as natural occurrences; this tendency is further exacerbated by the social distance among the races (Cortese 2006). "Social distance refers to the degrees of understanding, acceptance, and intimacy that usually typify personal and social relations, especially between ethnic or racial groups" (Cortese 2006:8). When the stereotypes are extremely negative, there is usually greater social distance (Cortese 2006). Finally, group identification refers to dividing people into groups; in societies that are more unequal, group identification can lead to an "us" versus "them" mentality. Cortese (2006) argues that cultural transmission, social distance, and group identification are all used to justify not only the unequal manner in which the American justice system is allowed to operate, but how discriminating language and stereotypes are used to maintain the *status quo*. Language and stereotypes are another method to "socially control members of subordinate groups" (Cortese 2006:10).

These theories outline the struggle between the dominant group and the subordinate group, but they do not explain the actual public policy process. The arguments thus far described must be put into the specific context of the concrete development of governmental policies.

---

[73] "In sounding this theme, Douglas used anecdotal and statistical evidence to demonstrate that the death penalty in the United States was visited disproportionately upon the 'poor, young, and ignorant' and upon 'the Negro, and the members of unpopular groups" (Steiker and Steiker 1995: 367).

Therefore, the integrated theory to be employed for this study must explain the entire process from sociological roots to public policies and programs. To this end, an overview of Kingdon's garbage can model is provided to explain how public policies are developed, legislatively adopted and ultimately implemented. This model will be combined with the previous discussion of conflict theory and power-threat theory to formulate the overall analytical framework used for this study.

Public Policy Theory

In his garbage can model, Kingdon (2003) argues that the manner in which policies are adopted and implemented is not, as Lindblom (1950) argues, uniformly incremental but is oftentimes the result of a coupling of three streams that eventually lead to the passage of new policy. The three streams consist of problems, policies, and politics (Kingdon, 2003). "[T]he logical structure of such a model is (1) the flow of separate streams through the system, and (2) outcomes heavily dependent on the coupling of the streams – couplings of solutions to problems; interactions among participants; the fortuitous or purposeful absence of solutions, problems, or participants – in the choices (the garbage cans) that must be made" (Kingdon, 2003:86). It is important for policy entrepreneurs to recognize when these streams merge to form "windows" through which policies can be debated, modified, and adopted. In terms of death penalty legislation, the politics stream includes state-level socio-demographic factors such as education, race, homicide rates, and poverty rates. The problem stream consists of the level of homicide rates. Finally, the policy stream takes into account the adoption and implementation of death penalty statutes.

INTEGRATED SOCIOLOGICAL POLICY THEORY

As shown in the Figure 5, this integrated framework takes into account *Social Conditions* that may have an effect on the decision-making process of policy formation. Within this theoretical model, there is also a connection between the three converging streams. Often the *Social Conditions* will have an influence on a society's politics as well as the problems that the society faces. In terms of applying this model to factors that may influence capital punishment implementation, high

Figure 5: Framework based on an Integrated Sociological Policy Model

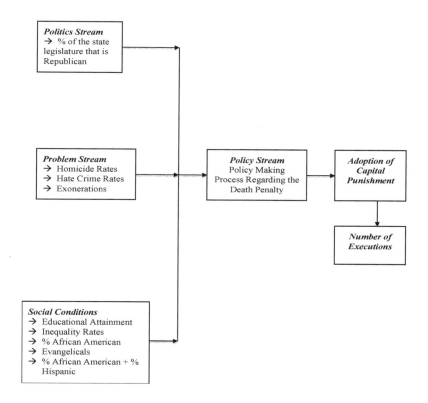

poverty rates may lead a state to become more conservative (as measured by the percentage of the state legislature that is Republican), whereas high educational attainment rates may result in a more liberal population. Evangelicals tend to be conservative and vote for Republicans, thus increasing the likelihood of a state having the death penalty and implementing it. Hate crimes, like homicide rates, are more likely to predict a higher probability in a state having a death penalty statute and in performing executions. Conversely, exonerations highlight the problem death penalty statutes have in some states, and thus would decrease the likelihood a state has the death penalty and implements it. In addition, states having a higher percentage of African Americans are more likely to be conservative because minority groups are seen as a threat.

This model shows factors that the research literature leads us to believe could explain the differences in adoption and implementation of the death penalty between states. This is important in terms of the social, political, and economic landscape of each state. Of course, there may be some lawmakers that want to appear to comply with their constituents' preference for the death penalty, but who write the legislation in such a way that it allows for few death sentences to be issued by courts and few actual executions to take place. Conversely, there may be some legislators that support capital punishment and want to prove to their voters that they can indeed get tough on crime and criminals. Finally, lower numbers of executions may reflect the changing social, economic, and political climate of a state. States with a troubled history with the death penalty tend to have lower levels of social inequality (i.e., low poverty rates) and thus will be less likely to perform executions.

CHAPTER 5
Research Questions and Hypotheses

The implementation of the death penalty varies greatly by state. This study will attempt to explain these differences in terms of the characteristics identified as salient in the empirical and theoretical literature pinched at the state-level. Some the questions to be addressed are as follows: Are the differences among the states the result of *Social Conditions*, such as poverty and education, and racial composition, such as levels and percentage African-American? Do the *political leanings, religion, and regional location* of the states explain why some states execute and others do not? Do *crime rates*, in terms of homicide rates and hate crimes, have an effect on the implementation of death penalty statutes? The following hypotheses will be tested at the bivariate and multivariate level:

Politics Stream Hypothesis #1: *States where Republicans are the majority of the state legislature are more likely to adopt capital punishment and to have a higher number of executions than states where Democrats are the majority of the state legislature.*

As noted previously, Nice (1992) stated that research has found that states that are more conservative are more likely to have the death penalty. Republicans are more inclined to support strict criminal laws and harsh punishments for crimes. Mitchell and Sidanius (1995:608) found that political conservatism was "consistently related to execution use." It follows it is important to not only determine if a state has the death penalty, but also to document how many executions are carried

85

out each year. If this hypothesis is supported by the data, it would provide one form of confirming evidence for social control and social dominance theories.

Social Conditions Hypothesis #1: *States with lower levels of educational attainment (in terms the percentage of the population with a high school diploma) are more likely to adopt capital punishment and to perform more executions.*

Educational attainment has often been used as part of socioeconomic status (SES). Those with a lower SES tend to have a lower social value. Therefore, as a function of SES, educational attainment may implicate social inequality as the underlying cause of the social problem faced in states with capital punishment. If this hypothesis is supported by my findings, it would provide evidence for social control and social dominance theories. People of lower socioeconomic status may be seen as inherently more dangerous and more likely to commit crime, thus resulting in the adoption of harsher punishments by dominant social groups.

Social Conditions Hypothesis #2: *States with higher inequality rates are more likely to adopt capital punishment and to perform more executions.*

Mitchell and Sidanius (1995:603) also found that "social hierarchy in a state was positively associated with the number executed in a state."[74] Accordingly, this study examines not only the inequality rates of the state, but its poverty rates as well. Although both variables may have an effect on the death penalty, particularly since they measure similar factors, the strength of the correlation of a particular factor can illuminate other problems within a state besides high crime rates.

---

[74] These authors controlled for "membership in the Old Confederacy, the degree of violent crime, political conservatism, state income, state population size, population density, degree of education, the proportion of whites, and the proportion of white crime victims" (Mitchell and Sidanius 1995: 603).

Social Conditions Hypothesis #3: *States with a higher percentage of African Americans are more likely to adopt capital punishment and perform more executions.*

Nice (1992) mentions in his study that states with a higher percentage of African Americans are more likely to have the death penalty. Arguably, this could be the result of the racial threat that harks back to the days of *Reconstruction* in the United States. Although African Americans are less likely to support capital punishment, their political and economic resources tend to not be as great as white Americans. The fear of the African American male by middle class white Americans allows politicians to support and adopt capital punishment, particularly in states where the racial composition is more evenly split between whites and blacks. If this hypothesis is supported by the analysis, social conflict and social dominance theories would be supported. In addition, Cortes' theory on cultural transmission would also be supported, because the social distance (i.e., segregation) in American social life creates an "us" versus "them" mentality, allowing whites to support a punishment that is more likely to be imposed on African Americans.

Social Conditions Hypothesis #4: *States with a higher percentage of Evangelicals are more likely to adopt capital punishment and perform more executions.*

Evangelicals tend to be more conservative in their political views than other religious denominations. Layman (1997:288) found in his review of American National Election Studies data from 1980 to 1994 that "members of evangelical denominations [are] becoming increasingly Republican relative to their counterparts in mainline denominations." As noted previously, Republicans tend to be more conservative and to support the concept of capital punishment. Consequently, states with a higher percentage of Evangelicals would tend to be more likely to adopt and implement the death penalty. If the null hypothesis is rejected, this hypothesis would support the tenets of social dominance theory.

Problem Stream Hypothesis #1*: States with higher homicide rates are more likely to adopt capital punishment and to perform more executions.*

Nice (1992) notes that states with higher violent crime rates are more likely to have the death penalty. These violent crime rates include homicide and property crimes involving persons such as armed robery. As a result, the population may have an increased apprehension about their safety, which results in severe punishments for all crimes, but homicides in general.

Problem Stream Hypothesis #2*: States with higher hate crime rates are more likely to adopt capital punishment and to perform more executions.*

As noted previously, lynchings were often used after the Civil War as a means of social control. Today there has been an increased discussion of "hate crimes," which encompass not just crimes committed against African Americans but also committed against marginalized and vulnerable populations in general.[75] As a result, there is an increased acceptance of the fact that some crimes are committed as a way of subjugating or instilling fear in marginalized populations. Most hate crimes include violence against people as a result of their race, religion, or sexual orientation. Consequently, hate crimes can be seen as serving the same purpose that lynching did in the past, i.e., as a means of exerting social control by using violence. If the present analysis supports this hypothesis, then social dominance and social control theories would be supported as well. However, if states do not consider hate crimes as serious, they may not report and prosecute them, in which case there may be no association with executions.

---

[75] "A hate crime is a traditional offense like murder, arson, or vandalism with an added element of bias. For the purposes of collecting statistics, Congress has defined a hate crime as a "criminal offense against a person or property motivated in whole or in part by an offender's bias against a race, religion, disability, ethnic origin or sexual orientation." Hate itself is not a crime—and the FBI is mindful of protecting freedom of speech and other civil liberties." (FBI N.D.)

Problem Stream Hypothesis #3*: States with more exonerations are less likely to adopt capital punishment and to perform more executions.*

As noted previously on the topic of innocence and the death penalty the act of executing an innocent person when broadcast widely to the public can change public opinion. Therefore, the more a state's population is made aware of innocent persons being convicted and executed in their state, the less likely will be the implementation of capital punishment.

CHAPTER 6

Methodology

The majority of the data for this study is drawn from the U.S. Census Bureau. As a result, decennial and semi-decennial estimate data were collected from these sources for 1985, 1990, 1995, 2000, 2005, and 2009. The data from all 50 states were combined into one data set, and panel data methods are employed to investigate change over time.

Bruderl (2005) argues that there are many benefits to analyzing panel data. First, panel data are more informative and more efficient than replicated cross-sectional studies. According to Bruderl (2005:2), there is "more variability, less collinearity, and more degrees of freedom" using this method. Second, he (2005:2) notes that panel data allow researchers "to study individual dynamics" which could facilitate the understanding of cohort effects and time on the impact of specific variables of interest. Third, panel data can add to our understanding of cause and effect or "the time-ordering of events" (Bruderl 2005:2). Finally, panel data allow researchers "to control for individual unobserved heterogeneity" (Bruderl 2005:2).[76]

According to Dougherty (2006:408), this last strength is of particular interest to researchers and social scientists since heterogeneity bias is "a common problem in the fitting of models with cross-sectional data sets." Dougherty (2006:408) echoes Bruderl's opinion that the ability "to reveal dynamics that are difficult to detect with cross-sectional data" is an asset when analyzing data from many points in time. Finally, Dougherty (2006) highlights the additional benefit that panel data sets can feature large numbers of observations.

---

[76] "Heterogeneity Bias: The bias in OLS due to omitted heterogeneity (or omitted variables)" (Wooldridge 2000:796).

DATA AND SAMPLE

Table 2 sets forth a listing of the data sources for the several variables used in this study. The data for the political party composition of the state legislatures were collected from U.S. Census Bureau and The National Conference of State Legislatures. Data on percentage of the population with a high school diploma (educational attainment), inequality rates, the percentage of the population that is African American, and the percentage of the population that is Hispanic were collected from the U.S. Census Bureau. Data on homicide rates and hate crime rates were gathered from the FBI Uniform Crime Reports.

Table 2: Summary of Variables and Data Sources

CATEGORY	VARIABLE	SOURCE
Politics	Percentage of the state legislature that is Republican	U.S. Census Bureau and The National Conference of State Legislatures
Social Conditions	Educational Attainment	U.S. Census Bureau
	Inequality rates	U.S. Census Bureau
	Percent of population that is African American	U.S. Census Bureau
	Percent of population that is Hispanic	U.S. Census Bureau
	Evangelicals	The Association of Religion Data Archives
Problems	Homicide rates	FBI Uniform Crime Reports
	Hate Crime Rates	FBI Uniform Crime Reports
	Exonerations	Death Penalty Information Center

The Association of Religion Data Archives maintains state-level data on the religious dominations of each state. Finally, the Death Penalty Information Center maintains records of executions and exonerations for each state. Table 3 outlines the number of observations, mean, standard deviation, minimum value and maximum value for the 50 states. As noted in the table, data from the U.S. Census Bureau were not available for inequality rates and for educational attainment for 1985, this information is treated as missing data in the analysis. In addition, Nevada state legislators do not have a party affiliation.

Table 3: Number of Observations, Mean, Standard Devation, Minimum Value, and Maximum Value for States

Variable	Number of Observations	Mean	Standard Deviation	Minimum value	Maximum value
Inequality Rate	300	43.833	2.37	37.8	50.2
Educational Attainment*	300	81.008	7.203	58.9	92.3
% Black	300	10.559	9.402	.2	37.4
Homicide Rates	300	5.617	3.21	.6	17.2
Politics**	294	45.235	15.064	6	77
Hate Crime Rate	300	2.360	3.056	0	16.16
Exonerations	300	.417	1.071	0	8
Evangelicals	300	15.961	12.291	1.19	54.27
Executions	300	3.94	13.356	0	135
% Black + % Hispanic	300	17.75	11.913	.29	49.6
State Population Per Million	300	5.403	5.975	.36	36.96

Data was not available for 1985, therefore data available for 1980 and 1990 was averaged for the 1985 value
** The state legislature in Nevada does not elect delegates based on party affiliation*

VARIABLES AND MEASUREMENT

The political party composition of state legislatures, educational attainment, and each state's African American and Hispanic population are expressed as percentages and were obtained from the U.S. Census Bureau covering the years from 1985, 1990, 1995, 2000, 2005, and 2009. The educational attainment for each state is measured by the percentage of the total population 25 years and over with a high school diploma.

The economic inequality variable will be measured using the Gini coefficient from the U.S. Census Bureau. The "Gini coefficient is based on the Lorenz curve (the observed cumulative income distribution) and the notion of a perfectly equal income distribution" (U.S. Census Bureau 2005). The closer the ratio is to zero, the greater the equality a state enjoys; conversely, the closer the ratio is to one, the greater the inequality that can be found in that state. The U.S. Census Bureau (2005) utilizes the following formula to calculate the Gini coefficient (u represents the population mean, n is the weighted number of observations, and Xi represents the weighted income of an individual:

$$\text{GINI} = [(2/un^2)\sum(iXi)] - (n+1)/n$$

States with higher Gini coefficient should have a higher number of executions. The Gini coefficient was obtained from the U.S. Census Bureau for the following years: 1985, 1990, 1995, 2000, 2005, and 2009. The Gini coefficient was multiplied by 100 to create a percentage, making it easier to analyze and explicate findings in the discussion of the study results.

Data from the FBI Uniform Crime reports is used to compare the homicide rate and hate crimes rates for each state. The FBI provides reports for crime rates for these main classifications, which will allow for a state to state comparison. These rates will be expressed as a rate per 100,000 people.

Finally, executions and exonerations will simply be the number of executions carried out by the state. In addition to testing the concurrent effect on executions as a dependent variable, additional models using the independent variables lagged by five years are run to take into account the potential time delay on executions (See Table 2: Summary of Independent Variable and Data Sources).

In addition to the variables noted, region and year are included in the models as controls. Dummy variables are used for West, Midwest and Northeast.[77] The years 1985, 1990, 1995, 2000, 2005, and 2009

---

[77] There is a high correlation between the South and many of the independent variables being tested, including Evangelicals and homicide rates. As a

will also be noted as dummy variables. A combined term for race is included to test for any effects of the size of the minority population (% Black + % Hispanic).

Selection of Variables

The factors associated with the states' adoption and implementation of the death penalty are likely and diverse. In an attempt to add to existing research, I have explored a wide range of potential independent variables. First, poverty rates were excluded from the present study for two reasons: (1) poverty rates were highly correlated with executions; (2) inequality rates provide a better measurement for overall inequality, as opposed to overall poverty. In an attempt to include as many variables without sacrificing degrees of freedom, I decided to use inequality rates rather than poverty rates.

I considered gun ownership as a potential predictive variable but discarded it because several studies have found a high correlation between gun ownership and homicide rates (see Gius 2008; Miller, Azrael, and Hemenway 2002; Kleck 1979). Fear of crime and attitudes towards capital punishment were also considered. However, the costs to access these state-level data from General Social Survey (GSS) were prohibitive.

Finally, I considered the dissimilarity index provided by the U.S. Census Bureau to take segregation into account. Unfortunately, these data are only available for the largest metropolitan areas in each state, not as an overall "degree of segregation" in a state.

STATISTICAL ANALYSIS

Due to the fact that executions occur in only a few states (those that have the death penalty), a zero-inflated negative binomial regression model will be used (Mwalili, Lesaffre, and Declerck 2007). A zero-inflated negative binomial regression model is ideal for studies that involve a large number of zeros within the data (no death penalty and

---

result, this analysis will control for the other 3 major regions. In addition, the states were coded using the designation provided in the Death Penalty Information Center's state database.

no executions). "Zero-inflated regressions combine two models: one that focuses on the presence or absence of the outcome and a second that models the extent of the outcome when it is nonzero" (Atkins and Gallop 2007: 726).

This model will allow for an estimation of the two separate issues investigated in this study. First, this model takes into account that there is a difference between states with and without the death penalty (Jacobs and Carmichael 2004; Atkins and Gallop 2007). This model then also takes into account the fact that even if a state has the death penalty, there will be differences in implementation (Jacobs and Carmichael 2004; Atkins and Gallop 2007). "The zero-inflated model is suited for such conditions because it estimates two processes simultaneously: the likelihood of a zero value ...and the effect of the predictor variables on the non-zero-count of ..." (R. King 2008: 1372).[78]

According to R. King (2008:1372), "[n]egative binomial regression models include a parameter that allows the conditional variance of the dependent variable to exceed the conditional mean, thus providing more efficient and less biased estimates than the Poisson and OLS models. Coefficients in these models can be interpreted as the percentage change in the expected count of the dependent variable per unit change in the independent variable (Long 1997) by taking the antilog of the coefficient" (R. King 2008: 1372). Gardner, Mulvey and Shaw (1995:402) argue that this model "gives a more skeptical account of the certainty and value of the predictions than does the Poisson" (Gardner, Mulvey and Shaw 1995:402).

Therefore, the panel data general specifications in the present analysis will be:

$$\text{Executions} = b_0 + b_1 \% \text{ Black} + b_2 \text{ Inequality Rate}$$

---

[78] The methodology used for this study is the same as that used by Jacobs and Carmichael (2004). "We estimate with a zero-inflated negative binomial procedure (Cameron & Trivedi 1998; Long 1997) that uses two equations. One estimates the factors the produce zero scores while the other equation models the factors that produce integer counts above one" (Jacobs and Carmichael 2004:259).

$+ b_3$ Hate Crime Rate
$+ b_4$ Homicide Rate
$+ b_5$ Exonerations
$+ b_6$ Educational Attainment
$+ b_7$ Republican State Legislature
$+ b_8$ Evangelicals
$+ b_9$ 1985 $+ b_{10}$ 1990 $+ b_{11}$ 1995 $+ b_{12}$ 2000 $+$
b_{13} 2005$+ b_{14}$ 2009
$+ b_{15}$ West $+ b_{16}$ Midwest $+ b_{17}$ Northeast
$+ b_{18}$ % Black $+$ % Hispanic

A total of ten models will be estimated. Model 0 will be run twice: (1) it will test each of the hypotheses separately, i.e. each variable will be used alone as a predictor and inflated by the variable being tested and (2) it will be tested with the five-year lag noted above. All models will use state population as an exposure variable and will be clustered by state.

For Model 1, the following variables will be included in the regression model and will be used as inflation variables: African American percentage, inequality rates, hate crime rates, homicide rates, exonerations, educational attainment, Republican State Legislature, Evangelicals, years (except 2009), and regions (South is the reference). This model will also be run with the 5-year variable lag (Model 5).

For Model 2, all variables noted in Model 1 will be included in the regression except for region. All the variables noted in the regression portion of this model will also be used as inflation variables. This model will also be run with the 5-year variable lag (Model 6).

For Model 3, all the variables from Model 1 will be included except for the % Black variable. The race variable will be replaced with the % Black $+$ % Hispanic term. This will take into account potential issues related to racial population that may be deemed a threat. This model will also be lagged in Model 7. Model 4 will include the variables listed in Model 3 except region will be removed; this model will be lagged in Model 8.

"The use of exposure is superior in many instances to analyzing rates as response variables because it makes use of the correct probability distributions" (Statistical Consulting Group 2007). In this analysis, the use of state population per million variable as an exposure variable allows for the probability of the adoption and implementation of the death penalty while taking into account the size of the state population.

By clustering standard errors by the state variable, I take into account that there are 50 states and that the number of executions is not necessarily independent at each point (year) that is being analyzed. In other words, this analysis is not comparing 300 potential observations (50 states*6 years), but is looking at the effect of the independent variables across states and within states over the period of this study. These analyses take into account the differences between states with the death penalty and states without, and demonstrate the differences between states that have the death penalty but implement at varying degrees.

Finally, the predicted probability of having no execution as a function of each factor in each model, the predicted number of executions in states with at least one execution, and the predicted number of executions as a function of each variable will be graphed.

WEAKNESS OF PANEL DATA REGRESSION ANALYSIS

Panel data regression analysis is an excellent method to use when comparing events or changes in policy over time. However, the variables selected for analysis must make some transition during the period in question. As mentioned previously, the majority of executions take place in only a few states, consequently there is little change over time in most states.

In addition, Dougherty (2006) notes that there are three main drawbacks for using panel data analysis. "First, the intercept $\beta 1$ and any X variable that remains constant for each individual will drop out of the model. The elimination of the intercept may not matter, but the loss of the unchanging explanatory variables may be frustrating" (Dougherty 2006:412). As will be discussed in more detail below, the inability to include the regional variable may be problematic.

The second criticism of using panel data, according to Dougherty (2006:413) "is the potential impact of the disturbance term." Usually the disturbance term holds constant in the model. However, given the addition of time within this model, the disturbance term may not hold constant.

Finally, Dougherty (2006:413) argues that when there is an attempt to eliminate the unobserved effect, "we lose one degree of freedom for every individual in the sample" (Dougherty 2006:413). Thus, the model may be unduly constrained and could limit the predictive value of the model.

In terms of this analysis, these drawbacks can impact the eventual results. First, it is impossible to include region in this type of model. The zero-inflated binomial regression requires variables that change, even if minimally, over time. Region has been found to be a highly predictive variable in determining the adoption and implementation of capital punishment across states. Second, it is impossible to include every potential independent variable that may have an effect on the adoption and implementation of the death penalty. However, given the number of variables used in this analysis, there may still be an issue of constraining the parameters of our estimates.

Despite these drawbacks, this methodology best suit the data collected and the investigation of the research questions posed. The data employed in this study have many zeros, because there are many states that either do not have the death penalty or, even if they have the death penalty, perform no executions. The zero-inflated binomial regression model takes into account the subtle changes in data that have excessive zeros. In addition, the use of panel data analysis allows for the study of changes in each of the variables over time. These changes may have some explanatory power in determining which factors contribute to the changes in the adoption and implementation of capital punishment at different points in time.

CHAPTER 7

Results

The goal of this study is to explain the differences between states that have the death penalty and those that do not, and to explain as well the differences in the number of executions in states that employ capital punishment. In order to assess each research hypothesis posed in this study, each variable is used alone as a predictor and inflated by the variable being tested. As noted previously, population per million is utilized as an exposure variable and standard errors are clustered by state. The dependent variable is the number of executions. Table 4 has two panels; the top panel predicts the number of executions, while the lower panel predicts whether the states have the death penalty or not. A positive coefficient in the top panel signifies a positive correlation between the dependent and independent variables. However, a positive coefficient in the lower panel signifies a negative correlation between the dependent and independent variables. In addition, standard errors were clustered by state for all models featured in Table 4.[79] The numbers reported in parentheses are standard errors.

Politics Stream Hypothesis #1: *States where Republicans are the majority of the state legislature are more likely to adopt capital punishment and to have a higher number of executions than states where Democrats are the majority of the state legislature.*

---

[79] Note that only 49 states were clustered. Due to the fact that its state legislature is not separated by Republicans and Democrats, it was not possible to cluster the variables for Nevada.

Model 0 of Table 4 shows bivariate zero inflated binomial regressions for all variables. In Column 1, the percentage of the state legislature was the independent variable (Politics) and the number of executions in each state was the dependent variable, while using state population as an exposure variable and inflating using the politics variable. The results show that while there is a significant statistical correlation between politics and whether a state has the death penalty, it is not as expected (2.72; p≤.01). The lower the percentage of Republicans in the state legislature, the more likely the state is to have capital punishment. This may reflect the need by Democrats in certain states to adopt the "get tough on crime" rhetoric that Republicans have used for years. It appears that in the South, in order to get elected, politicians must embrace the adoption and implementation of the death penalty. However, this variable loses its statistical significance when the variables are lagged as shown in Table 5, Column 1, indicating that the current rather than previous composition of the legislature is important.

Social Conditions Hypothesis #1: *States with lower levels of educational attainment (in terms of the percentage of the population with a high school diploma) are more likely to adopt capital punishment and to perform more executions.*

Column 2 of Table 4 displays a bivariate zero inflated binomial regression for the percentage of the population that has earned their high school diploma for each state with the number of executions in each state as the dependent variable, while using state population as an exposure variable and inflating using the educational attainment variable. Although this regression demonstrates that educational attainment by itself (.032) is not statistically significant in explaining the differences in the number of executions carried out in each state, it is an important control variable for subsequent analyses because it is part of the measure for the socioeconomic status of the states' citizens. Education is statistically significant in explaining the adoption (.356; p≤.01) of capital punishment. When the variables are lagged, education continues to be statistically significant in predicting the adoption of capital punishment, as noted in Column 2 of Table 5.

Table 4: Model 0 – Bivariate Zero Inflated Binomial Regression of Each Variable (Standard Errors Clustered by State)[80]

	1	2	3	4	5	6
Politics	.014 (.013)					
Education		.032 (.026)				
Inequality			.141 (.123)			
% Black				.002 (.022)		
Evangelicals					.022 (.019)	
Homicide						-.072 (.050)
Politics	.272** (.096)					
Education		.356** (.150)				
Inequality			-.753* (.286)			
% Black				-.127*** (.039)		
Evangelicals					-.158*** (.040)	
Homicide						-.654*** (.178)
Log-likelihood	-520.3	-524.8	-515.9	-515.7	-503.3	-511.3
Chi^2	1.09	1.61	1.32	.01	1.38	2.06
Prob>chi2	.296	.204	.251	.914	.239	.151
N	294	300	300	300	300	300

* $p \leq .05$ ** $p \leq .01$ *** $p \leq .001$

[80] Region was not included in the bottom panel. When Model 0 was run with just region in both portions, there appeared to be a problem with collinearity. For previous runs of Model 0, please see Appendix D. The numbers reported in parentheses are standard errors.

Table 4 (cont'd): Model 0 – Bivariate Zero Inflated Binomial
Regression of Each Variable (Standard Errors Clustered by State)

	7	8	9	10	11
Hate Crimes	.060				
	(.060)				
Exonerations		.072			
		(.136)			
Midwest			-1.405***		
			(.533)		
Northeast			-2.224		
			(1.906)		
West			-1.830***		
			(.471)		
1985				-1.483*	
				(.650)	
1990				-.767	
				(.624)	
1995				-.600	
				(.581)	
2000				.071	
				(.577)	
2005				.088	
				(.617)	
% Black +					.002
% Hispanic					(.020)
Hate Crimes	-77.702***				
	(6.502)				
Exonerations		-18.468***			
		(1.170)			
1985				.154	
				(.877)	
1990				.112	
				(.897)	
1995				-12.132*	
				(5.594)	
2000				-28.408***	
				(2.664)	
2005				-.219	
				(.855)	
% Black +					-.114*
% Hispanic					(.041)
Log-likelihood	-523.3	-513.4	-507.4	-515.6	-515.7
Chi^2	.99	.28	19.42	31.91	.01
Prob>chi2	.319	.597	.000	.000	.904
N	300	300	300	300	300
* $p \le .05$	** $p \le .01$		*** $p \le .001$		

Social Conditions Hypothesis 2: *States with higher inequality rates are more likely to adopt capital punishment and to perform more executions.*

In Model 3 of Table 4, a zero inflated binomial regression was run whereby inequality rates were the independent variable and the number of executions in each state was the dependent variable, while using state population as an exposure variable and inflating using the inequality variable. As noted previously, inequality rates are measured by the Gini coefficient for each state; in addition, standard errors were clustered by state. This regression shows that this variable is significant in predicting the adoption capital punishment (-.753; $p \leq .01$). When the variables are lagged, inequality continues to be statistically significant in predicting the adoption of capital punishment, as noted in Column 3 of Table 5.

Social Conditions Hypothesis #3: *States with a higher percentage of African Americans are more likely to adopt capital punishment and to perform more executions.*

Column 4 of Table 4 uses race as measured by the percentage of the population that is African American as the independent variable. Race does not predict the number of executions in a state, but it is statistically significant in predicting the adoption of the death penalty in both non-lagged and lagged models (-.127; $p \leq .01$ and -.122; $p \leq .01$, respectively). In addition, the % Black + % Hispanic variable is statistically significant in explaining the adoption of capital punishment in Column 11 of Table 4 (-.114; $p \leq .01$). This effect indicates that the adoption of the death penalty among states varies with the percentage of the population that is African American and Hispanic, thereby supporting the social threat theory. This result holds for the lagged model (-.118; $p \leq .01$).[81]

---

[81] A curvilinearity variable was tested in terms of race. The results show that there is not a curvilinearity using the data presented in this study. For the results of that particular diagnostic test, please see Appendix G.

Social Conditions Hypothesis #4*: States with a higher percentage of Evangelicals are more likely to adopt capital punishment and to perform more executions.*

Column 5 of Table 4 shows the percentage of the population that is Evangelical as the independent variable. Although the presence of Evangelicals does not have a predictive value in explaining the differences in implementation of the death penalty, it does have a statistically significant effect on the adoption of capital punishment (-.158; p≤.001). The same finding holds true when variables are lagged by 5 years as shown in Column 5 in Table 5 (-.162; p≤.001).

Problem Stream Hypothesis #1*: States with higher homicide rates are more likely to adopt capital punishment and to perform more executions.*

Column 6 of Table 4 uses the number of homicides committed per 100,000 people as the independent variable. As hypothesized, the homicide rate is indeed a statistically significant predictor (-.654; p≤.001) of whether a state adopts the death penalty. However, as with the other variables used in this study, homicide rates by themselves do not explain the number of executions carried out. This trend is also demonstrated when the variables are lagged by 5 years, as shown in Column 6 of Table 5 (-.664; p≤.001).

Problem Stream Hypothesis #2*: States with higher hate crime rates are more likely to adopt capital punishment and to perform more executions.*

Column 7 of Table 4 uses the number of hate crimes committed per 100,000 people as the independent variable. As hypothesized, the number of hate crimes is a statistically significant predictor (-77.702; p≤.001) of whether a state adopts the death penalty. This effect is reversed when the variables are lagged by 5 years, as shown in Column 7 of Table 5 (26.915; p≤.001). This may reflect the fact that in order for a hate crime to be labeled as such, there needs to be sensitivity in the community to violent acts being the result of discrimination. Therefore, this result may be further evidence of discrimination given the fact that in some states hate crimes are rarely prosecuted as such.

Table 5: Model 0 – Bivariate Zero Inflated Binomial Regression of Each Variable (Standard Errors Clustered by State and Lagged by 5 Years)[82]

	1	2	3	4	5	6
Politics	-.003 (.012)					
Education		.009 (.026)				
Inequality			.187 (.122)			
% Black				.008 (.024)		
Evangelicals					.029 (.019)	
Homicide						-.020 (.053)
Politics	.080 (.214)					
Education		.239* (.113)				
Inequality			-.664** (.280)			
% Black				-.122** (.043)		
Evangelicals					-.162*** (.043)	
Homicide						-.664*** (.137)
Log-likelihood	-468.2	-472.0	-466.1	-466.5	-451.2	-466.5
Chi^2	.05	.11	2.34	.11	2.32	.11
Prob>chi2	.818	.744	.126	.737	.128	.737
N	245	250	250	250	250	250
* p≤.05		** p≤.01		*** p≤.001		

[82] The numbers in parentheses are standard errors. For the results of previous runs of the models, please see Appendix E and Appendix F.

Table 5 (cont'd): Model 0 – Bivariate Zero Inflated Binomial Regression of Each Variable (Standard Errors Clustered by State and Lagged by 5 Years)

	7	8	9	10	11
Hate Crimes	.074 (.089)				
Exonerations		.112 (.189)			
Midwest			-1.409** (.542)		
Northeast			-2.291 (1.768)		
West			-1.827*** (.470)		
1985				-1.447** (.462)	
1990				-.731 (.450)	
1995				-.561 (.346)	
2000				.109 (.300)	
% Black + % Hispanic					.002 (.022)
Hate Crimes	26.915*** (.954)				
Exonerations		-17.756*** (.715)			
1985				.235 (.713)	
1990				.193 (.771)	
1995				-11.980** (4.792)	
2000				-26.153*** (2.418)	
% Black + % Hispanic					-.118** (.049)
Log-likelihood	-471.0	-465.4	-506.5	-516.0	-466.6
Chi^2	.70	.35	19.51	30.57	.01
Prob>chi2	.401	.552	.000	.000	.935
N	250	250	300	300	250

* $p \leq .05$ ** $p \leq .01$ *** $p \leq .001$

Problem Stream Hypothesis #3: *States with more exonerations are less likely to adopt capital punishment and to perform more executions.*

Exonerations are measured as the number of adjudicated and convicted people later found to be innocent in the state. As Column 8 of Table 4 demonstrates, this variable is not associated with the number of executions carried out but is statistically significant with relation to the adoption of capital punishment (-18.468; p≤.001). This effect is also found when the variables are lagged by 5 years as shown in Column 8 of Table 5 (-17.756; p≤.001).

Other Variables Tested – Time and Place

As noted previously, region is an important factor to take into account when analyzing capital punishment. As Column 9 in Table 4 show, the Midwest and West are negatively correlated with executions (-1.405; p≤.001 and -1.830; p≤.001 respectively) as compared to the South.[83] After lagging the variables 5 years, this trend hold the same – the Midwest and West is still less likely to carry out executions than the South (-1.409; p≤.01 and -1.827; p≤.001, respectively)

In Column 10 of Table 4, differences between the years of the analysis were tested. In 1985 there were significantly fewer executions than in 2009 (-1.483; p≤.05) and both 1995 and 2000 were statistically significantly higher than 2009 in the adoption of the death penalty (-12.132; p≤.05 and -28.408; p≤.001, respectively). In Column 10 of Table 5, both 1995 and 2000 were statistically significantly higher in the adoption of the death penalty than 2005 (-11.980; p≤.01 and -26.153; p≤.001, respectively). Finally, 1985 had significantly fewer executions than in 2005 (-1.483; p≤.01).

In sum, the bivariate analyses show a relatively consistent pattern in association. In both the lagged and non-lagged models only year (1985 fewer than the latest year) and region (Midwest and West fewer than South) affect the number of executions. In the non-lagged model (Table 4) all variables are significantly associated with having the death

---

[83] Region was not included in the inflation portion of the model due to an issue with collinearity.

penalty, including the combined race variable. In the lagged model (Table 5), the effect of politics is no longer statistically significant.

Multivariate Analyses

Table 6 presents zero inflated multiple regression models using the following non-lagged variables: inequality rates, education, percent African American, homicide rates, politics, hate crime rates, Evangelicals and exonerations. These were also used as inflation variables. State population per million was used as an exposure variable and standard errors were clustered by state. Model 1 (Column 1) is testing the basic multivariate model. Controlling for all other factors in the model, the years 2000 (1.104; $p \leq .05$) and 2005 (1.87; $p \leq .05$) are statistically significant predictors of executions. In 2000 and 2005 there were significantly more executions than in 2009. Interestingly, the bottom panel of the table shows that exonerations (-1.422; $p \leq .05$) were marginally significant in predicting the adoption of the death penalty.

In Model 2 (Column 2) in Table 6, I tested the effect of region on the basic model. The results show that hate crime rates (.256; $p \leq .01$), Evangelicals (.049; $p \leq .01$) and the years 2000 (1.226; $p \leq .05$) and 2005 (1.328; $p \leq .001$) were significant in predicting executions. In terms of death penalty adoption, homicide rates (-.550; $p \leq .05$) gain statistical significance, while exonerations (-1.638; $p \leq .05$) retain their statistical significance.

Table 6 Model 3 presents the results for the model using the combined race variable (%Black + % Hispanic). In this model, only the year 2005 (2.92; $p \leq .01$) is significant in predicting the number of executions. However, the combined race variable (-2.13; $p \leq .05$) is statistically significant in explaining the adoption of the death penalty, thereby supporting the social control/social threat theories.

Model 4 of Table 6 test the same variables as those demonstrated in Model 3, but region has been removed. Once again, the year 2005 (4.12; $p \leq .001$) is statistically significant in predicting the implementation of the death penalty. Once region is removed, hate crimes (2.54; $p \leq .01$) and Evangelicals (2.08; $p \leq .05$) become significant. This result remains consistent in both Model 2 and in Model 4, which may be due to the fact that both variables are correlated with the South and thus serves as a proxy for the region variable. In addition, Evangelicals (-2.10; p≤.05) and exonerations (-1.93; p≤.05) are statistically significant in predicting the adoption of the death penalty. The combined race variable (-1.87; p≤.06) is only marginally significant.

Model 5 in Table 7 tests the basic model, but the variables are lagged by 5 years. The Midwest (-2.26; p≤.05) and the West (-3.19; p≤.001) are significant in predicting the number of executions, while homicide rates (-1.92; p≤.05), hate crime rates, (-2.28; p≤.05), and Evangelicals (-2.07; p≤.05) are significant in predicting the adoption of capital punishment.

Model 6 in Table 7 tests the basic model without region and lags the variables by 5 years. When not controlling for region, homicide rates are no longer predictive of the adoption of the death penalty. Hate crime rates (-2.19; p≤.05) and Evangelicals (-1.92; p≤.05) continue to be predictive of the odds of adopting the death penalty.

Model 7 in Table 7 tests the combined race variable and the variables are lagged by 5 years. The West (-2.71; p≤.01) is the only variable that is significant in relation to the number of executions, while hate crime rates (-2.18; p≤.05) and Evangelicals (-3.04; p≤.01) continue to be significant in relation to the adoption of the death penalty. The combined race term is not significant in this lagged model.

Model 8 in Table 7 tests the combined race variable without controlling for region and is lagged by 5 years. Once again, hate crime rates (-1.96; p≤.05) and Evangelicals (-2.29; p≤.05) retain their statistical significance in relation to the adoption of the death penalty.[84]

---

[84] In order to examine the relationships in Tables 6 and 7 in more depth, it is important to determine the predicted probability of a state (1) not having an execution as a function of the independent variables listed; (2) the predicted number of executions in states that have had at least one execution; and (3) the predicted number of executions as a function of the independent variables tested in this analysis. This analysis is reported in Appendix H.

Table 6: Zero Inflated Binomial Regression Estimates of the Number of Executions in the States in 1985, 1990, 1995, 2000, 2005, and 2009 (Clustered by State)[85]

	1 (Not Lagged)	2 (Not Lagged)	3 (Not Lagged)	4 (Not Lagged)
Politics	.009 (.037)	.021 (.021)	.032 (.038)	.021 (.020)
Education	.007 (.082)	-.025 (.074)	-.074 (.148)	-.043 (.094)
Inequality	.000 (.0155)	.111 (.131)	.025 (.137)	.107 (.136)
% Black	-.025 (.021)	.006 (.024)	---	---
Evangelicals	.030 (.022)	.049** (.020)	.021 (.021)	.046* (.022)
Homicide	-.043 (.097)	-.065 (.075)	-.012 (.124)	-.066 (.075)
Hate Crime	.162 (.103)	.256** (.104)	.120 (.123)	.246** (.097)
Exonerations	-.045 (.075)	.000 (.091)	.022 (.092)	-.006 (.084)
Midwest	-.904 (.541)	---	-1.001 (.746)	---
Northeast	-.787 (3.065)	---	.722 (3.463)	---
West	-1.740 (1.131)	---	-1.281 (.818)	---

---

[85] The number in parentheses are standard errors.

Table 6 (cont'd): Zero Inflated Binomial Regression Estimates of the Number of Executions in the States in 1985, 1990, 1995, 2000, 2005, and 2009 (Clustered by State)

	1 (Not Lagged)	2 (Not Lagged)	3 (Not Lagged)	4 (Not Lagged)
1985	.692 (1.358)	1.131 (1.333)	-.565 (2.641)	.786 (1.538)
1990	1.256 (.988)	1.633 (.906)	.312 (2.127)	1.395 (1.083)
1995	.695 (.584)	.971 (.547)	.305 (1.130)	.910 (.644)
2000	1.104* (.562)	1.226* (.526)	.711 (.986)	1.135 (.617)
2005	1.087** (.366)	1.328*** (.331)	1.120** (.384)	1.367*** (.332)
% Black + % Hispanic	---	---	-.028 (.045)	-.002 (.028)
Politics	.021 (.042)	-.004 (.040)	.010 (.048)	.002 (.039)
Education	.027 (.146)	-.003 (.142)	-.126 (.240)	-.042 (.163)
Inequality	.465 (.396)	.657 (.425)	.688 (.412)	.720 (.442)
% Black	-.049 (.069)	-.065 (.054)	---	---
Evangelicals	-.053 (.046)	-.057 (.051)	-.1120 (.067)	-.089* (.042)
Homicide	-.494 (.276)	-.550* (.283)	-.405 (.326)	-.438 (.351)

Table 6 (cont'd): Zero Inflated Binomial Regression Estimates of the Number of Executions in the States in 1985, 1990, 1995, 2000, 2005, and 2009 (Clustered by State)

	1 (Not Lagged)	2 (Not Lagged)	3 (Not Lagged)	4 (Not Lagged)
Hate Crime	-.025 (.126)	.028 (.156)	-.097 (.162)	-.046 (.155)
1985	4.811 (2.771)	5.970* (3.192)	2.672 (2.347)	4.255 (2.725)
1990	4.088 (2.332)	4.954 (2.796)	-2.175 (2.121)	3.374 (2.600)
1995	.886 (1.110)	1.017 (1.112)	-.342 (1.162)	.242 (1.213)
2000	-.564 (1.140)	-.807 (1.242)	-1.740 (1.309)	-1.425 (1.375)
2005	.810 (1.297)	1.030 (1.136)	1.147 (1.533)	.953 (1.322)
% Black + % Hispanic	---	---	-.114* (.053)	-.082* (.044)
Log-Likelihood	-450.4	-455.6	-448.6	-454.7
Chi2	128.97	59.36	73.95	49.95
Prob >Chi2	.000	.000	.000	.000
N	294	294	294	294
*p≤.05	*p≤.01	***p≤.001		

Table 7: Zero Inflated Binomial Regression Estimates of the Number of Executions in the States in 1985, 1990, 1995, 2000, 2005, and 2009 (Clustered by State)[86]

	5 (Lagged)	6 (Lagged)	7 (Lagged)	8 (Lagged)
Politics	-.035 (.026)	-.016 (.025)	-.029 (.032)	-.021 (.029)
Education	.004 (.054)	-.047 (.071)	.018 (.101)	-.014 (.099)
Inequality	-.261 (.152)	-.215 (.216)	-.198 (.206)	-.217 (.263)
% Black	-.051 (.030)	.004 (.029)	---	---
Evangelicals	.007 (.022)	.035 (.022)	.007 (.024)	.040 (.025)
Homicide	-.092 (.083)	-.106 (.099)	-.096 (.090)	-.127 (.101)
Hate Crime	-.117 (.087)	-.050 (.107)	-.079 (.097)	-.037 (.101)
Exonerations	.073 (.124)	.261 (.161)	.176 (.142)	.260 (.158)
Midwest	-.1.492* (.660)	---	-1.302 (.760)	---
Northeast	-2.009 (1.364)	---	-1.652 (1.823)	---
West	-2.433** (.763)	---	-1.904** (.702)	---

[86] The numbers in parentheses are standard errors.

Table 7 (cont'd): Zero Inflated Binomial Regression Estimates of the Number of Executions in the States in 1985, 1990, 1995, 2000, 2005, and 2009 (Clustered by State)

	5 (Not Lagged)	6 (Not Lagged)	7 (Not Lagged)	8 (Not Lagged)
1985	---	---	---	---
1990	-1.473 (.952)	-1.727 (1.393)	-1.045 (1.555)	-1.269 (1.603)
1995	-1.152 (.952)	-1.158 (1.133)	-.691 (1.333)	-.752 (1.301)
2000	.552 (.501)	.383 (.636)	.558 (.770)	.588 (.712)
2005	.232 (.388)	-.001 (.520)	.274 (.516)	.132 (.578)
% Black + % Hispanic	---	---	-.013 (.045)	.013 (.038)
Politics	.273 (.182)	-.255 (.189)	-.273 (.214)	-.2631 (.1901)
Education	-.465 (.274)	-.445 (.346)	-.420 (.318)	-.3826 (.4531)
Inequality	.994 (.962)	-.880 (1.170)	-.950 (1.613)	-.908 (1.432)
% Black	-.098 (.108)	-.103 (.113)	---	---
Evangelicals	-.280* (.136)	-.282* (.147)	-.294* (.097)	-.288* (.126)

Summary of Findings in Relation to Hypotheses

Politics Stream Hypothesis #1*: States where Republicans are the majority of the state legislature are more likely to adopt capital punishment and to have a higher number of executions than states where Democrats are the majority of the state legislature.*

This hypothesis was not consistently supported by the data. The non-lagged bivariate analysis revealed a statistically significant relationship between politics and adoption of the death penalty (2.84; $p \leq .01$), but this relationship was not as strong in subsequent models.

Social Conditions Hypothesis #1*: States with lower levels of educational attainment (in terms of years of the percentage of the population with a high school diploma) are more likely to adopt capital punishment and to perform more executions.*

The relationship between education and the adoption of the death penalty was not consistent across models. As predicted, the lagged and non-lagged bivariate analysis revealed a negative relationship between education and the adoption of the death penalty. However, the non-lagged and lagged multivariate models did not show a significant correlation. Therefore this hypothesis was not supported by the analysis.

Social Conditions Hypothesis #2*: States with higher inequality rates are more likely to adopt capital punishment and to perform more executions.*

Inequality rates were found to be statistically significant in the lagged and non-lagged bivariate models in relation to the adoption of the death penalty, but they appear to lose their significance when combined with other variables in multivariate models. Therefore, this hypothesis was not supported by the data.

Social Conditions Hypothesis #3*: States with a higher percentage of African Americans are more likely to adopt capital punishment and to perform more executions.*

The bivariate models (lagged and non-lagged) revealed a statistically significant relationship between % Black and the adoption of the death penalty. This relationship was not present in subsequent models. The data show that there is a statistically significant relationship between the combined race variable and the adoption of capital punishment in the non-lagged models, but this relationship does not appear in the lagged models. The data support the adoption of the death penalty portion of the hypothesis for the non-lagged models only, and thus support social control and social dominance theories. The data also reflect the complexity of the issue of race in relation to the adoption of the death penalty.

Social Conditions Hypothesis #4: *States with a higher percentage of Evangelicals are more likely to adopt capital punishment and to perform more executions.*

The bivariate analysis for both lagged and non-lagged models demonstrated that there was a positive correlation between Evangelicals and the adoption of the death penalty. The influence of this variable remained consistent in the lagged multivariate analysis, but this relationship is not evident in the non-lagged models. Therefore, the data is not consistent enough to support this hypothesis.

Problem Stream Hypothesis #1: *States with higher homicide rates are more likely to adopt capital punishment and to perform more executions.*

Homicide rates were shown to be statistically significant in the lagged and non-lagged bivariate analyses. This variable remained statistically significant in Models 2 and 7. As a result, this hypothesis was not supported by the results.

Problem Stream Hypothesis #2: *States with higher hate crime rates are more likely to adopt capital punishment and to perform more executions.*

As with homicide rates, hate crime rates were statistically significant in predicting the adoption of the death penalty in the bivariate analyses.

Interestingly, while the variable for hate crime rates was statistically significant in predicting the adoption of the death penalty in the lagged models, it was also statistically significant in predicting the number of executions when not controlling for region in the non-lagged models. The results are consistent enough to support this hypothesis.[87]

Problem Stream Hypothesis #3: *States with more exonerations are less likely to adopt capital punishment and to perform more executions.*

Exonerations were found to be statistically significant in relation to the adoption of the death penalty in both versions of the bivariate analysis. This variable remained statistically significant in the multivariate analyses of Models 1, 2, and 4. Therefore, this hypothesis was not consistent enough to support the hypothesis.

Other Variables Tested – Time and Place

As mentioned previously, in previous research on the death penalty time and place have been found to be extremely important variables. Previous research has focused mainly on the effect the South has in determining which states have the death penalty and which states carry out the most executions. This analysis took into account the differences in the Northeast, Midwest and West relative to the South. The bivariate analyses revealed that the Midwest and West had significantly fewer executions than the South in the lagged models. The bivariate analyses also showed that in 2000 there were significantly more executions than in 2009 in Models 1 and 2. In addition, there were significantly more executions in 2005 than in 2009 in the non-lagged models. Results for individual years were not consistent across models.

---

[87] One caveat to keep in mind is the fact that hate crime rates are somewhat subjective. It is up to the prosecutor to determine that a crime should be classified as a hate crime.

CHAPTER 8

Conclusion

The goal of this study was to determine what factors account for state variation in the adoption of the death penalty, and determine why some states implement it more than others in terms of executions carried out. I used a theoretical framework that included factors related to the Politics Stream, the Problem Stream, and the Social Conditions Stream to examine the policy making outcomes involving the death penalty across U.S. states over the period 1985 to 2009. The key research questions guiding the empirical analysis were as follows:

1. What are some of the political and social factors that determine state-level variation in the adoption of capital punishment and the number of executions between 1985 and 2009?
2. Is there a correlation between the adoption and the implementation of the death penalty and the political affiliation of a state?
3. When controlling for political and demographic factors, is adoption and implementation of capital punishment a response to homicide rates?

Given how complex the death penalty issue is in American society, no single explanation can be used to determine why some states have it or why others execute more people than the rest. However, the results of this analysis add another pixel to the emerging picture of the adoption and the implementation of capital punishment in the United States.

Homicide rates do have an effect on the adoption of the death penalty in the bivariate analysis, but they do not have the same effect when controlling for the African American population, extent of Republican Party presence in the state legislature, inequality rates, Evangelicals, exonerations, region, education, and years. This finding may indicate that capital punishment is not necessarily a reaction to high crime rates as measured by homicide rates. Instead, politicians and the public may be reacting to other social issues when labeling the problem as crime. As determined by other researchers, the death penalty may have been adopted as a result of fear of crime rather than the actual level of crime in some communities (Archer et al. 1983; Tyler and Weber 1982; Rankin 1979).

Percent African American population was also a highly correlated variable in predicting the adoption of capital punishment in the bivariate analysis. The results of the bivariate analysis and three of the four multivariate analyses support previous research (Jacobs et al. 2007; Cortese 2006; Jacobs, Carmichael, and Kent 2005; McAllister 2003; Lofquist 2001-2002; Tabak 1999; Baldus et al. 1998; Dieter 1998; Stevenson and Fredman 1994; Galliher at al 1992; United States General Accounting Office 1990; Tushnet 1989; Kennedy 1988; Hartung 1952). In addition, the results support the findings of Galliher et al. (1992:541) who found that "states with the highest concentrations of non-white citizens ha[d] used the death penalty most frequently." Those results also support the contention of Galliher and Galliher (1997), who found that the population racial composition is a predictive factor in the adoption of the death penalty. Of particular significance are the results of Models 3 and 4, which included the combined race variable (% Black + % Hispanic). These results suggest that race is an important factor when studying the death penalty and that its impact is more complex than previously reported.

The results of this study show that even though politics had a positive effect on the adoption of the death penalty in the bivariate analysis, the effect was not significant in the multivariate analysis. Previous researchers have found that states that tend to vote Republican also tend to have the death penalty (Stucky, Heimer, and Lang 2005; Jacobs and Carmichael 2002; Mitchell and Sidanius 1995; Nice 1992). The result regarding politics comes as no surprise given the fact that more executions take place in the South and, moreover, states in the

South tend to vote Republican. In order for Democrats to compete in states with capital punishment, they may have to adopt a similar rhetoric as that touted by Republicans.

The bivariate analysis of education and adoption of the death penalty revealed a negative correlation, but in the multivariate analyses the correlation was mixed. The education result is difficult to explain. The original hypothesis supposed that the higher the education, the more likely states are to reject capital punishment as an appropriate response to crime. The results from this analysis run counter to previous research (Newport 2007; Young 1991; Tyler and Weber 1982). This may point to the necessity to measure education in a different way. For example, including the percentage of the population with a college degree may support previous research. Using this measure of education may take into account class as well, since education is used as part of socioeconomic status.

The present study shows that inequality rates per se (Gini coefficient) are not a statistically significant factor in the multivariate analysis in explaining why some states have the death penalty. A state's racial composition appears to be more significant in the adoption of the death penalty than economic inequality.

Researchers have long established that disadvantaged populations in the United States are more likely to be sentenced to death. Hartung (1952) notes that African Americans, the poor, and the less educated are more likely to be sentenced to death. This is the logical result of prejudices and stereotypes about these groups as being more dangerous than whites, the wealthy, and the better educated. As Galliher and Galliher (1997:371) mention, higher levels of racial and ethnic heterogeneity and social and economic inequality are "associated with higher levels of interpersonal and intergroup conflict." This often leads to calls for harsher punishments (Galliher and Galliher 1997). Nice (1992) also mentioned that the poor are at a greater risk of being sentenced to death, which is due in part to the lower value we place on their lives in comparison to those of more prosperous citizens. It may also be a function of the lack of empathy affluent citizens for the poor (Nice 1992). Finally, the poor are less likely to have the resources to afford an adequate defense in court (Nice 1992).

Politicians argue that getting tough on crime requires capital punishment, but there is the potential that the death penalty is used when there is a strain on social order (Nice 1992: 1039). The analysis in the study supports this idea. Homicide rates were positively correlated with the adoption of the death penalty in the bivariate analysis. The data seem to suggest that politicians are willing to support the death penalty in proposing new legislations or amending pre-existing ones, but the actual implementation of such legislation does not necessarily follow suit.

In addition, given that the stakeholders closest to the actual process of the death penalty tend to oppose it – e.g., the American Medical Association, the American Bar Association, the American Nurses Association among others – it may be time to review the data of death penalty studies to determine whether this policy is indeed warranted and sustainable in the U.S. In other words: "The providers in the system who see themselves as providing a valuable service to a population in great need, but who will not be party to execution, will leave the prison environment, thereby reducing the pool of available professionals" (Weisbuch, 1984:309).

The present analysis supports the finding that the death penalty is adopted not as a result of social learning but rather as a result of citizens' fear of crime (Mooney and Lee 1999a). According to Mooney and Lee (1999a), morality policies, such as capital punishment, must be "de-moralized" and expressed as a solution to a problem if change is to take place. Although the "problem" that is supposedly being addressed is crime, the present study suggests that the underlying problem actually may be discrimination and racism. The overrepresentation of minority groups living at or below the poverty level contributes to the social threat others may feel about this socially and economically disadvantaged group.

In addition, many opponents to the death penalty have argued that the death penalty is more likely to be imposed on those least likely to be able to defend themselves, i.e. the poor and the uneducated. However, the results reported in this study may demonstrate that despite this fact, exonerations do seem to play some role in making states aware of this troublesome issue; both race and income tend to play a major role in wrongful convictions.

Although this analysis lacked statistical support for some of the hypotheses tested, the results were most interesting. Previous research noted the correlation of race and the death penalty. However, inequality, educational attainment and race are closely intertwined. Those with higher educational attainment are less likely to experience inequality (as measured by the Gini coefficient). Minority groups are more likely to suffer as a result of inequality. Therefore, educational attainment and race should continue to be included in analyzing why states adopt and implement the death penalty. It might be more fiscally sound to address the underlying issue, which is racial inequality as opposed to crime. Any policy that is designed to address the issue of racial inequality ought to include education as a social component and inequality among minority groups.

As mentioned previously, there are some noteworthy issues related to using panel data analysis. Dougherty (2006) identified three main criticisms of this type of analysis. First, independent variables that remain constant will drop out of the model. Second, there "is the potential impact of the disturbance term" (Dougherty 2006:413). Given the addition of time within this model, the disturbance term may not hold constant. Third, there is a loss of "one degree of freedom for every individual in the sample" (Dougherty 2006:413). Thus, the model may be unduly constrained, which limits its predictive value.

One other limitation to state-level analyses is the inability to assess county-level variations. Harris County in Texas, Baltimore County in Maryland, and Los Angeles County in California are just three examples of counties in individual states that send more people to death row than all the other counties in their states combined. Taking into account the differences not only between states, but within states as well, may provide a clearer picture of what is driving the cross-state differences in the number of executions. This would also address the issue of capturing the dominant local ideology, such as local Democratic representation, the percentage of the population that votes Democratic, and the influence of minorities in decision making.

The results from this study have opened the door for further studies to explain why some states adopt and implement the death penalty. Previous studies have mentioned that the poor are more likely to be charged and sentenced to death than their wealthier counterparts. A study examining this discrepancy would further elucidate the theories espoused here.

The results of this study show that the measures used may not be sufficiently sophisticated. Other state-level variables such as income per capita, welfare rates, and unemployment, for example, would may be helpful additions. As mentioned previously, there is some evidence that public opinion influences policy makers in the adoption and implementation of some types of policies. A measure for the states populations' support for the death penalty might improve the model when combined with some or all of the variables analyzed here.

In addition, introducing an index variable for political affiliation and for socioeconomic status (educational attainment, race, and income per capita) for each state may yield results that could support the hypotheses outlined in this study. Capturing a higher level of education (college graduates as opposed to high school graduates) may be more relevant to the questions posed here.

Additionally, a fear of crime proxy should be included in future research to test the hypothesis that the fear of crime, not necessarily crime itself, compels citizens and politicians to support the death penalty. Recidivism rates and prison population rates may have an influence on a community's fear of crime. Because the death penalty is largely argued in the courtroom, a variable that captures the difficulty in overturning death sentences at the state-level may explain the differences in the implementation of the death penalty.

Finally, the lagging of variables was an important component of the analyses presented in this study. Although it is difficult to determine the proper amount of time to lag, it is recommended for future research because many of the variables analyzed likely will not have an immediate impact. Time is a complex issue when determining the effect and impact of state-level variables on the adoption and implementation of the death penalty.

The data analyzed here suggest that there may be some systematic inequities in the adoption and implementation of the death penalty across states. The factors related to these inequities may highlight the idea that despite the Supreme Court's attempt at making the death penalty more consistent and consequently constitutional, the resulting legislation has thus far not resulted in similar punishments being meted out for similar crimes. Additionally, given the number of moratoriums and repeals of death penalty statutes taking place across the country, these results may further bolster the argument that states are not just reacting to murder rates, but are influenced by other factors. These factors include, but are not limited to, cost, exonerations, and the lack of deterrence. I believe that there will always be some states that will support their death penalty statutes (Texas and Florida being among them), but they appear to be becoming part of a small minority, especially as life sentences become available to juries. The current system may be argued as being little more than a lottery system, just as the Supreme Court argued when then-existing death penalty statutes were struck down forty years ago in *Furman*.

Appendix A: Capital Offenses by State, 2006

State	Offense
Alabama	Intentional murder with 18 aggravating factors (Ala. Stat. Ann. 13A-5-40(a)(1)-(18))
Arizona	First-degree murder accompanied by at least 1 of 14 aggravating factors (A.R.S. § 13-703(F))
Arkansas	Capital murder (Ark. Code Ann. 5-10-101) with a finding of at least 1 of 10 aggravating circumstances; treason.
California	First-degree murder with special circumstances; train wrecking; treason; perjury causing execution.
Colorado	First-degree murder with at least 1 of 17 aggravating factors; first-degree kidnapping resulting in death; treason.
Connecticut	Capital felony with 8 forms of aggravated homicide (C.G.S. 53a-54b).
Delaware	First-degree murder with at least 1 statutory aggravating circumstance.
Florida	First-degree murder; felony murder; capital drug trafficking; capital sexual battery.
Georgia	Murder; kidnapping with bodily injury or ransom when the victim dies; aircraft hijacking; treason.

State	Offense
Idaho	First-degree murder with aggravating factors; aggravated kidnapping; perjury resulting in death.
Illinois	First-degree murder with 1 of 21 aggravating circumstances.
Indiana	Murder with 16 aggravating circumstances (IC 35-50-2-9).
Kansas	Capital murder with 8 aggravating circumstances (KSA 21-3439, KSA 21-4625).
Kentucky	Murder with aggravating factors; kidnapping with aggravating factors (KRS 32.025).
Louisiana*	First-degree murder; aggravated rape of victim under age 13; treason (La. R.S. 14:30, 14:42, and 14:113). *Revision*: Revised the definition of aggravated rape as a capital-eligible offense to include any offense involving victims under age 13. (2006 La. Sess. Law, Act 178), effective 8/15/2006.
Maryland	First-degree murder, either premeditated or during the commission of a felony, provided that certain death eligibility requirements are satisfied.
Mississippi	Capital murder (97-3-19(2) MCA); aircraft piracy (97-25-55(1) MCA).
Missouri	First-degree murder (565.020 RSMO 2000).
Montana	Capital murder with 1 of 9 aggravating circumstances (Mont. Code Ann. § 46-18-303); aggravated sexual intercourse without consent (Mont. Code Ann. § 45-5-503).
Nebraska	First-degree murder with a finding of at least 1 statutorily-defined aggravating circumstance.

State	Offense
Nevada	First-degree murder with at least 1 of 15 aggravating circumstances (NRS 200.030, 200.033, 200.035).
New Hampshire*	Six categories of capital murder (RSA 630:1, RSA 630:5). *Revision*: Amended the capital statute to increase the minimum age of eligibility for a death sentence from 17 to 18 years at the time the offense was committed (N.H. Rev. Stat. Ann. 630:1,V), effective 1/1/2006.
New Jersey	Murder by one's own conduct, by solicitation, committed in furtherance of a narcotics conspiracy, or during commission of a crime of terrorism (NJSA 2C:11-3c).
New Mexico	First-degree murder with at least 1 of 7 statutorily-defined aggravating circumstances (Section 30-2-1 A, NMSA).
New York	First-degree murder with 1 of 13 aggravating factors (NY Penal Law §125.27).
North Carolina	First-degree murder (NCGS §14-17).
Ohio	Aggravated murder with at least 1 of 10 aggravating circumstances (O.R.C. secs. 2903.01, 2929.02, and 2929.04).
Oklahoma*	First-degree murder in conjunction with a finding of at least 1 of 8 statutorily-defined aggravating circumstances; sex crimes against a child under 14 years of age. *Revision*: Added as a capital offense sex crimes against a child under 14 years of age when the offender has a previous conviction for a similar offense (Okla. Stat. Ann. 10 § 7115), effective 7/1/2006.

State	Offense
Oregon	Aggravated murder (ORS 163.095).
Pennsylvania	First-degree murder with 18 aggravating circumstances.
South Carolina*	Murder with 1 of 12 aggravating circumstances (§ 16-3-20(C)(a)); criminal sexual conduct with a minor with 1 of 9 aggravators (§ 16-3-655). *Revision*: Added as a capital offense second and subsequent offenses of first-degree criminal sexual conduct with a minor who is less than 11 years of age (§16-3-655). Lawmakers also added as an aggravating factor murder committed by a person deemed a sexually violent predator under South Carolina law (§16-3-20(C)(a)(12). Both changes were effective 7/1/2006.
South Dakota*	First-degree murder with 1 of 10 aggravating circumstances. *Revision*: Amended the definition of aggravated kidnapping to eliminate death as a possible sentence (SDCL 22-19-1), effective 7/1/2006.
Tennessee	First-degree murder with 1 of 15 aggravating circumstances (Tenn. Code Ann. § 39-13-204).
Texas	Criminal homicide with 1 of 9 aggravating circumstances (TX Penal Code 19.03).
Utah	Aggravated murder (76-5-202, Utah Code Annotated).
Virginia	First-degree murder with 1 of 13 aggravating circumstances (VA Code § 18.2-31).
Washington	Aggravated first-degree murder.
Wyoming	First-degree murder.

* Revised statutory provisions relating to the death penalty during 2006.
(Department of Justice 2006)

Appendix B: Date of Capital Punishment Legislation Enactment

State	Date of Adoption
Alabama	5/3/1976
Alaska	N/A
Arizona	8/9/1973
Arkansas	3/23/1973
California	1/1/1974
Colorado	1/1/1975
Connecticut	12/1/1973
Delaware	3/29/1974
Florida	12/8/1972
Georgia	3/28/1973
Hawaii	N/A
Idaho	7/1/1973
Illinois	7/1/1974
Indiana	5/1/1973
Iowa	N/A
Kansas	4/22/1994
Kentucky	1/1/1975
Louisiana	7/2/1973
Maine	N/A
Maryland	7/1/1975
Massachusetts	N/A
Michigan	N/A

State	Date of Adoption
Minnesota	N/A
Mississippi	4/23/1974
Missouri	9/28/1975
Montana	3/1/1974
Nebraska	4/20/1973
Nevada	7/1/1973
New Hampshire	1/1/1991
New Jersey	8/6/1982
New Mexico	7/1/1979
New York	9/1/1995
North Carolina	6/1/1977
North Dakota	N/A
Ohio	1/1/1974
Oklahoma	5/17/1973
Oregon	12/7/1978
Pennsylvania	3/26/1974
Rhode Island	N/A
South Carolina	7/2/1974
South Dakota	1/1/1979
Tennessee	2/27/1974
Texas	1/1/1974
Utah	7/1/1973
Vermont	N/A
Virginia	10/1/1975
Washington	11/4/1975
West Virginia	N/A
Wisconsin	N/A
Wyoming	2/28/1977

Appendix C:

Correlations of the Independent Variables

	Poverty	Inequality	Education	Race	Homicide	Politics
Poverty	1.0	--	--	--	--	--
Inequality	.5168	1.0	--	--	--	--
Education	-.5034	-.2668	1.0	--	--	--
Race	.3603	.5389	-.4219	1.0	--	--
Homicide	.4917	.4201	-.6186	.6568	1.0	--
Politics	-.2763	-.03517	.4432	-.2651	.3456	1.0

N=245

Appendix D

Model 0 - Zero Inflated Binomial Regression of Each Variable (Standard Errors Not Clustered by State)

	1	2	3	4	5	6
Politics	1.42 (.0139)					
Inequality		.83 (7.9398)				
Education			.02 (.0004)			
Poverty				-0.44 (-.0172)		
Race					.28 (.0041)	
Homicide						-1.54 (-.0633)
Politics	1.48 (.2770)					
Inequality		2.11 (-73.0853)				
Education			-2.14** (.3101)			
Poverty				-2.98** (-.3116)		
Race					-4.05*** (-.1265)	
Homicide						-3.82*** (-.6578)
Log-likelihood	-520.1	-469.5	-469.5	-521.9	-515.5	-511.3
Chi^2 e^b	3.35	.70	.00	.19	.08	2.13

*p≤.05   ** p≤.01   ***p≤.001

137

Appendix E

Zero Inflated Binomial Regression Estimates of the Number of Executions in States in 1985, 1990, 1995, 2000, 2005, and 2009 (Standard Errors Not Clustered by State)

	1	2	3
Poverty	-.33	-.03	-.70
	(-.0194)	(-.0019)	(-.0401)
Inequality	1.08	1.47	1.95*
	(12.2068)	(17.9996)	(22.1064)
Education	-.55	-.47	-.25
	(-.0203)	(-.0183)	(.009)
Race	.89	.70	.93
	(.0167)	(.0142)	(.0174)
Homicide	-1.73	-2.00	-1.76
	(-.1117)	(-.1288)	(-.1111)
Politics	.65	.51	.35
	(.0081)	(.0064)	(.0043)
Poverty	-1.78	------	-2.27*
	(-.2091)		(-.3028)
Inequality	------	.97	1.75
		(19.8405)	(37.4173)
Race	-.78	-1.13	-1.16
	(.0398)	(-.0626)	(-.0665)
Homicide	-2.27**	-1.76	-2.36
	(-.4871)	(-.5933)	(-.6295)
Log-Likelihood	-448.1	-449.3	-446.2
Chi2	6.87	8.32	9.29

*p≤.05   ** p≤.01   ***p≤.001

Appendix F

Table 11: Zero Inflated Binomial Regression Estimates of the Number of Executions in the States in 1985, 1990, 1995, 2000, 2005, and 2009

	1
Poverty	2.59**
	(.1416)
Inequality	-1.37
	(-12.5021)
Education	1.14
	(.418)
Race	3.31***
	(.0659)
Homicide	-.30
	(-.0203)
Politics	2.91**
	(.0352)
Poverty	-0.00
	(-72.6135)
Inequality	-0.00
	(-3068367)
Education	-0.00
	(-67.4229)
Race	-0.00
	(97.6388)
Homicide	-0.00
	(-148.7291)
Politics	-0.00
	(-33.8791)
Log-Likelihood	-448.1
Chi2	6.87

*p≤.05   ** p≤.01   ***p≤.001

141

Appendix G

Table 12: Test for the Curvilinearity Related to Race

	Model 1	Model 2
Education	.004 (.075)	-.015 (.074)
Homicides	-.050 (.109)	-.054 (.080)
Politics	.008 (.038)	.019 (.021)
Hate Crimes	.151 (.102)	.275** (.104)
Exonerations	-.049 (.079)	-.012 (.091)
Evangelicals	.027 (.027)	.049* (.020)
Inequality	-.002 (.158)	.105 (.129)
% Black	-.058 (.125)	.067 (.076)
% Black^2	.001 (.003)	-.002 (.002)
1985	.624 (1.384)	1.202 (1.246)
1990	1.220 (1.022)	1.661* (.847)
1995	.710 (.617)	1.661 (.847)
2000	1.102* (.565)	1.221* (.512)
2005	1.104**	1.269**

Appendix H: Predicted Probabilities

Politics and the Death Penalty

As noted in Tables 6 and 7, the relationship between the death penalty and politics is not clear or consistent. Figure 6 shows the predicted probability of having executions as a function of politics for Model 0, not lagged and lagged. The data from the model which was not lagged shows a more pronounced slope than the lagged model. However, in Figure 7 the relationship between politics and executions is mixed. Model 1 shows a steady decrease as the percentage of Republicans in state legislature increase, while Model 3 shows a positive relationship.

Figure 6

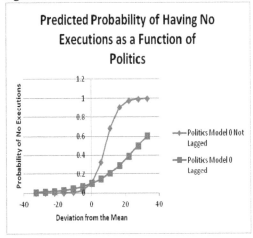

Figure 7

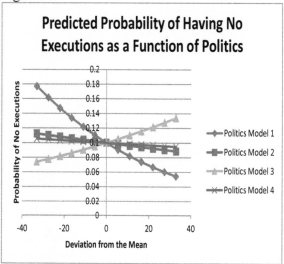

The lagged models resulted in a consistent negative relationship between politics and executions, as shown by the steep slope in Figure 8. As noted previously, this negative relationship may be the result of Southern Democrats' support for law and order policies. These figures illustrate the mixed relationship between politics and executions.

Figure 8

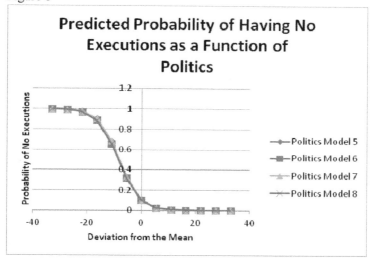

Figures 9, 10 and 11 show the relationship between the predicted number of executions in states with at least 1 execution. Again, the relationship is mixed in Models 0, not lagged and lagged (as illustrated in Figure 9). Figures 10 and 11 show a more consistent relationship among the lagged and not lagged models.

Figure 9

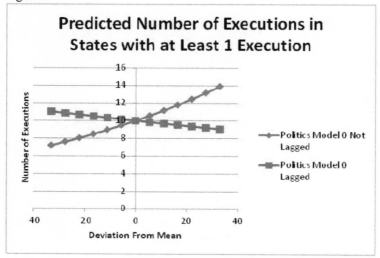

However, Models 1-4 have a positive relationship between politics and the predicted number of executions in states with at least 1 execution (Figure 10), while Models 5-8 shows a negative relationship (Figure 11).

Figure 10

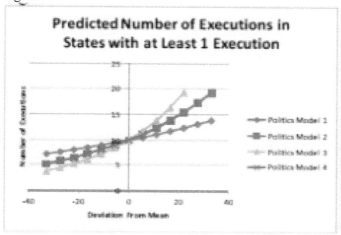

Figure 11

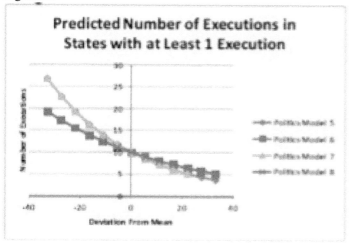

Figures 12, 13, and 14 represent the predicted number of executions as a function of politics. In Figures 12 and 14, the predicted number of executions decreases as values deviate from the mean.

Figure 13, however, shows a gradual increase. Interestingly, the slopes on Figure 13 and in Figure 14 are similar within the graphs, but comparing the two graphs demonstrates the lack of consistency with regards to the relationship between executions and politics.

Figure 12

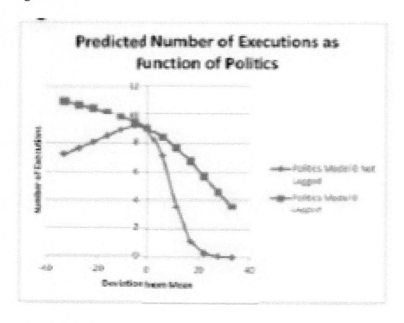

Figure 13

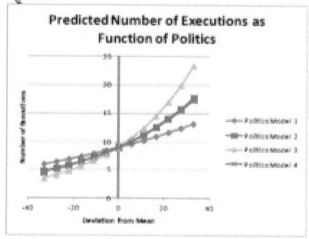

Figure 14

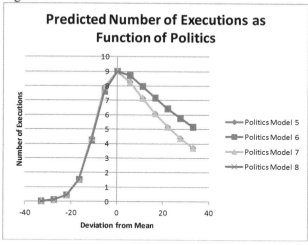

Education and the Death Penalty

Figures 15, 16, and 17 show the predicted probability of having no executions as a function of education. As with politics, the relationship between education and executions is not consistent in the present analysis. Figure 15 shows a positive relationship between executions and the probability of having no executions, which supports the hypothesis noted previously.

Figure 15

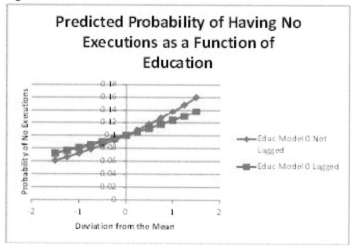

However, Figure 16 shows only a slight increase in Models 1, 2, and 4, while Model 3 shows a notable decrease. Figure 17 demonstrates the negative relationship between education and the noted predicted probability. As noted previously, the addition of education in these models is important as it is part of the socioeconomic status measurement of each state.

Figure 16

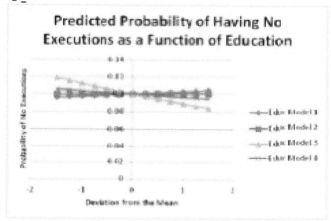

Figure 17

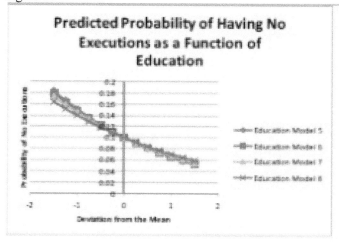

Figures 18, 19, and 20 show the predicted number of executions in states with at least one execution. Again, the relationship between executions and education is mixed. Figure 18 shows a positive relationship, while Figure 19 and 20 do not present as clear of a picture.

It appears from these two figures that removing region from the models creates some consistency (as show by Models 2 and 4 in Figure 19 and Models 6 and 8 in Figure 20).

Figure 18

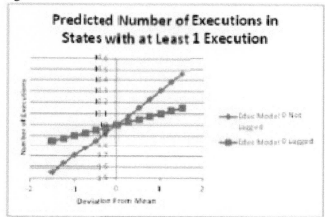

Figure 19

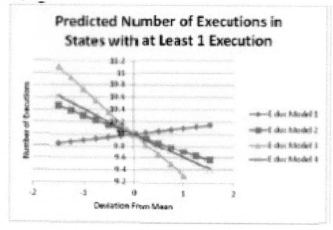

Figure 20

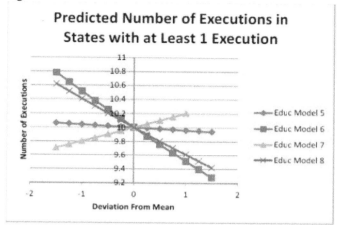

Figures 21, 22 and 23 show the predicted number of executions as a function of education. Once again, the relationship is not consistent across models. In the Model 0 results (both not lagged and lagged), there is a decrease in executions as the education of a state increases. However, in Figure 22, there is a decreasing slope in Models 1, 2, and 4, but an increasing slope in Model 3. Figure 23 shows a consistent relatively minimal increase across the lagged models. Taken together, these figures illustrate the complexity of education and the death penalty.

Figure 21

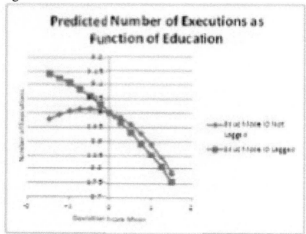

Figure 22

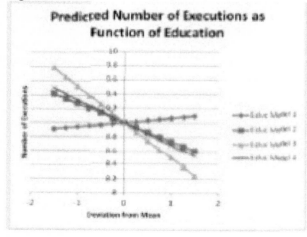

Figure 23

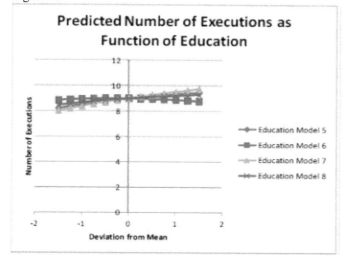

Inequality and the Death Penalty

Figures 24, 25, and 26 illustrate the predicted probability of having no executions as a function of inequality rates. Taking the figures separately, the slopes are consistent within each graph, with Figures 24 and 26 having a negative slope and Figure 25 having a positive slope. The results in Figures 24 and 26 are as predicted and supports the hypothesis related to inequality and the death penalty. However, Figure 25 refutes the hypothesis.

Figure 24

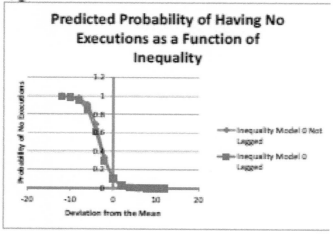

Figure 25

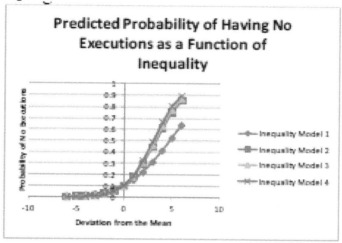

Figure 26

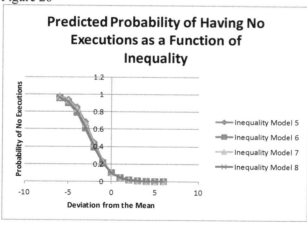

Figures 27, 28 and 29 show the predicted number of executions in states with at least one execution. Once again, the results are mixed. As predicted, there is a positive slope in Model 0 (lagged and not lagged) and in Model 1 and 2. However, the remaining models refute the hypothesis that an increase in inequality rates result in an increase in executions.

Figure 27

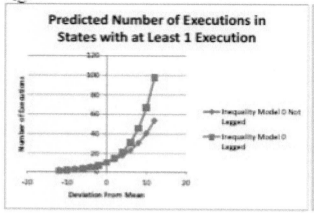

Figure 28

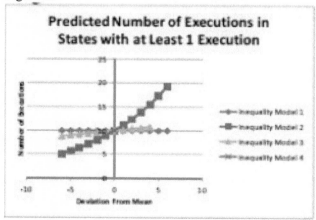

Interestingly the slope is almost exactly the same in the models shown in Figure 29. Thus, the lagging of variables seems to create a more consistent outcome than the non-lagged models.

Figure 29

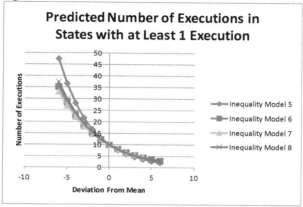

Figures 30 – 32 illustrate the predicted number of executions as a function of inequality rates. Figures 31 and 32 shows more consistency than the previous graphs, but they are still markedly different than Figure 30. These findings refute the hypothesis related to inequality rates and executions.

Figure 30

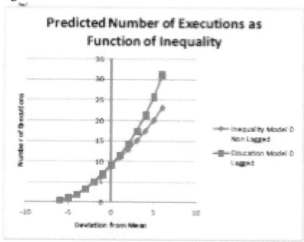

Figure 31

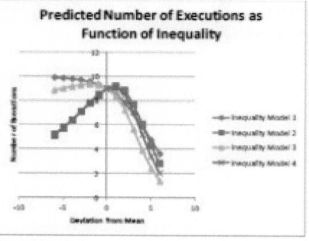

Figure 32

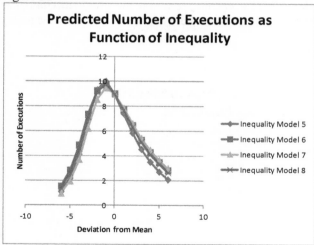

Race and the Death Penalty

Figures 33 and 34 demonstrate the predicted probability of having no executions as a function of the percentage of the population that is Black. These show a consistent finding that the probability of having no executions decreases as the percentage of the population that is Black increases. These results support the hypothesis related to race.

Figure 33

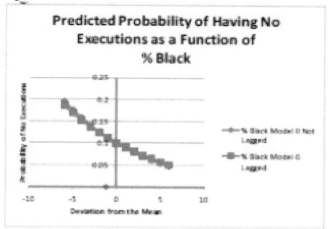

Figure 34

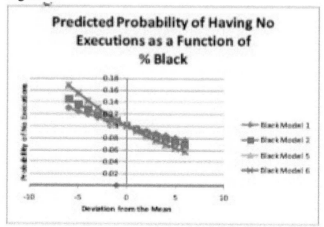

Figures 35 and 36 show the predicted number of executions in states with at least one execution. The results for the models are mixed. Figure 35 shows that the lagged model has a steeper slope than the non-lagged, while region seems to change the direction of the correlation as shown in Figure 36. The relationship appears to be negative when controlling for region (Models 1 and 5) and positive when not controlling for region (Models 2 and 6).

Figure 35

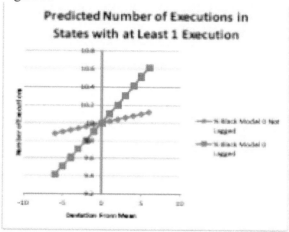

Figure 36

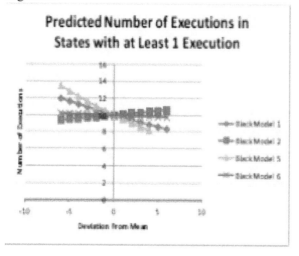

Figures 37 and 38 illustrate the predicted number of executions as a function of the percentage of the population that is Black. Consistent with Figures 35 and 36, Figures 37 and 38 show a positive relationship in Model 0 (lagged and non-lagged) and in Models 2 and 4. These results suggest that region does have an influence on the results and the relationship between race and executions.

Figure 37

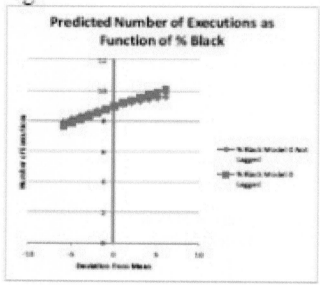

Figure 38

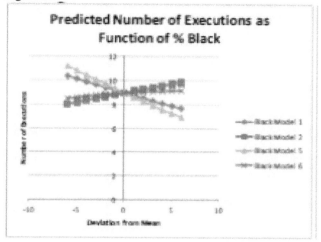

Figures 39, 40 and 41 illustrate the predicted probability of having no executions as a function of percentage of the population that is Black + percentage of the population that is Hispanic. Model 0 (lagged and non-lagged) and Models 3 and 4 shows the predicted negative relationship between race and executions. Models 7 and 8, however, show a positive relationship.

168

Appendices

Figure 39

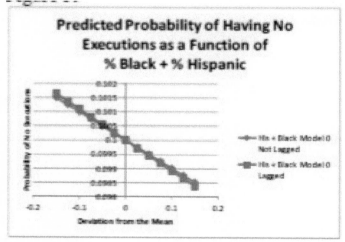

Figure 40

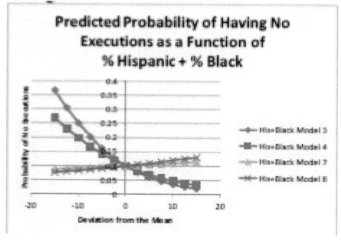

Figures 41 and 42 illustrate the predicted number of executions in states with at least one execution. The lagged and non-lagged models follow the same positive slope. However, Models 3, 4, 7, and 8 are not consistent. This may be the result of the complexity of race in America generally, and within the criminal justice system specifically. These results refute the hypothesis related to race.

Figure 41

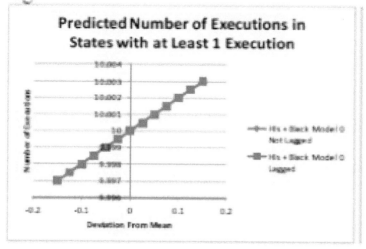

Figure 42

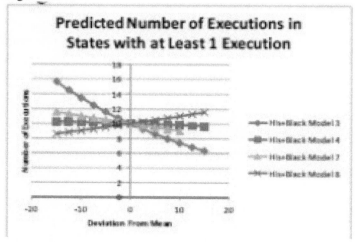

Figures 43 and 44 shows the predicted number of executions as a function of the percentage of the population that is Black plus the percentage of the population that is Hispanic. Once again Model 0 (lagged and non-lagged) have the same slope, while Model 3, 4, 7, and 8 show differing slopes. Region appears to be a significant factor in these models, since the models controlling for region have a negative slope, while those not controlling for region has a positive slope. Therefore, region seems to be more significant and influential than race in these analyses.

Figure 43

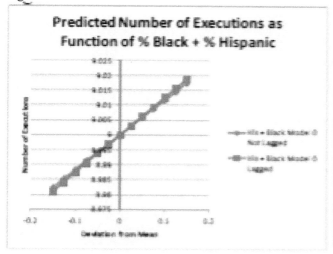

Figure 44

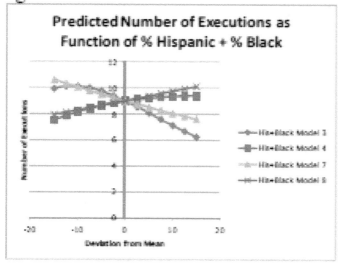

Evangelicals and the Death Penalty

Figures 45, 46, and 47 illustrate the predicted probability of having no executions as a function of Evangelicals. These graphs show some consistency across models when it comes to the influence of Evangelicals. The negative slope suggest that as the percentage of Evangelicals increase, the probability of having no executions decreases, which supports the hypothesis related to capital punishment and Evangelicals.

Figure 45

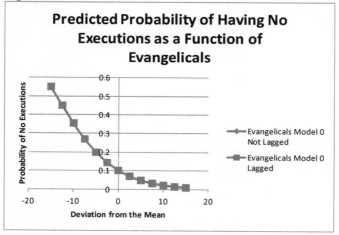

Figure 46

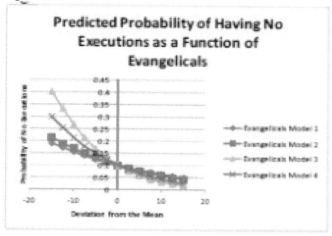

Figure 47

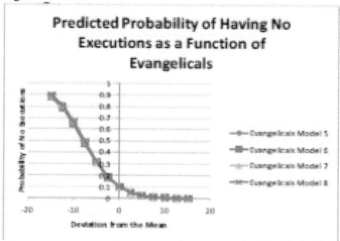

Figures 48, 49, and 50 illustrate the predicted number of executions in states with at least one execution. As with the previous discussion, the results are relatively consistent across models. There is a positive relationship between Evangelicals and executions. As Tables 6 and 7 showed, this relationship is not only consistent, but significant across models.

Figure 48

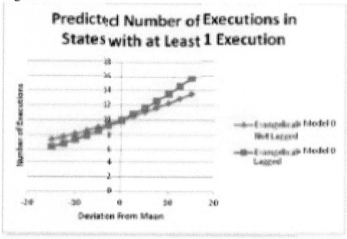

Figure 49

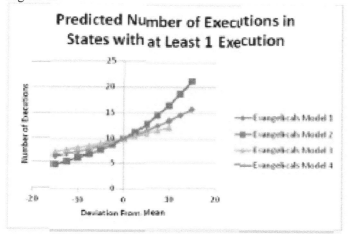

Figure 50

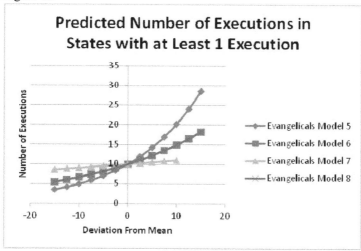

Figures 51, 52, and 53 show the predicted number of executions as a function of Evangelicals. As predicted, an increase in the percentage of Evangelicals results in an increase in the predicted number of executions across models.

Figure 51

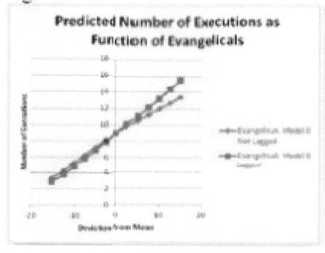

Figure 52

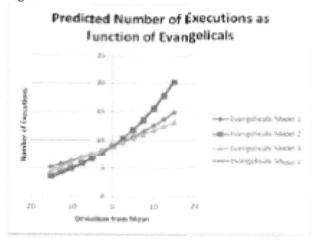

Figure 53

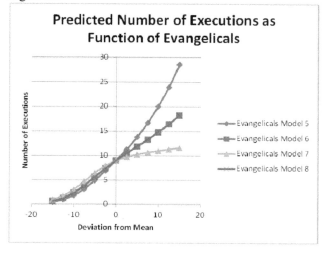

Homicide Rates and the Death Penalty

Figures 54, 55, and 56 illustrate the predicted probability of having no executions as a function of homicide rates. The results are consistent across models, but the relationship is not as predicted. These findings indicate that an increase in homicide rates result in a decreased probability of having no executions. This is not surprising given that homicide rates tended to have a significant correlation with the adoption and not necessarily the implementation of the death penalty.

Figure 54

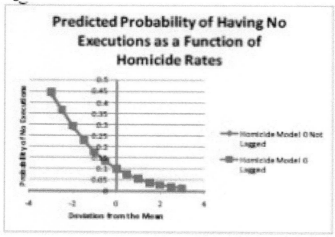

Figure 55

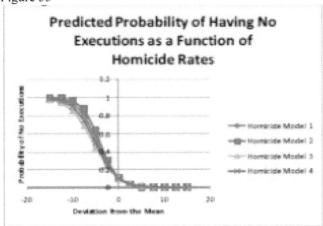

Figure 56

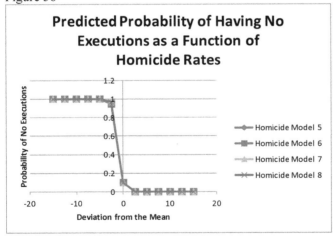

Figures 57, 58, and 59 illustrate the predicted number of executions in states with at least one execution. Once again, the results across the models are similar in slope, but contrary to what were hypothesized previously. The negative correlation suggests that homicide rates are not necessarily the driving force behind executions. Thus, the other variables in this study appear to have a more significant influence.

Figure 57

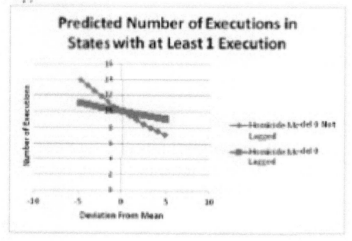

Figure 58

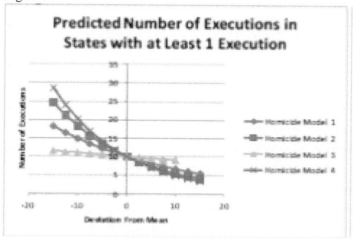

Figure 59

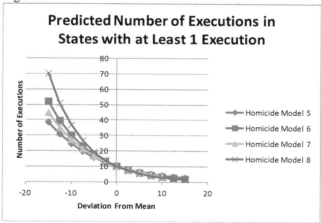

Figures 60, 61, and 62 show the predicted number of executions as a function of homicide rates. Interestingly, executions appear to reach a peak at the mean, then decrease as the deviation from the mean increases across all the models. This again suggests that crime is not the driving force behind the differences in the number of executions across states, thus supporting the theories of social control and social dominance.

Figure 60

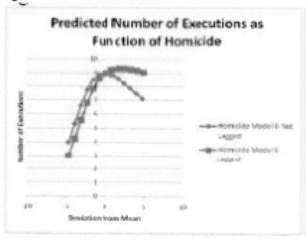

Figure 61

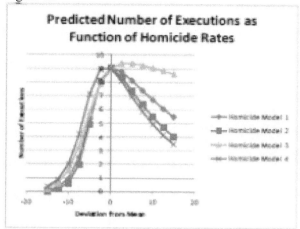

Figure 62

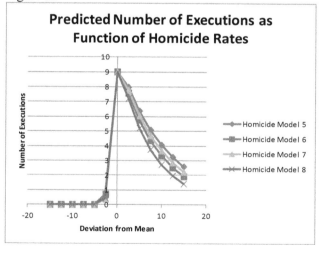

Hate Crime Rates and the Death Penalty

Figures 63, 64, and 65 illustrate the predicted probability of having no executions as a function of hate crime rates. The lagged and non-lagged models in Figure 63 shows a completely opposite relationship between executions and hate crime rates. Models 1 – 4 in Figure 64 also show mixed results, while Figure 65 shows that Models 5 – 8 are more consistent. This may be due to two factors. First, hate crimes are prosecuted in a subjective manner (i.e., one prosecutor may files hate crime charges in one case, while another with a similar set of facts may not). Second, the lagging of variables appears to have helped create more consistency, which in turn may be the result of the relatively recent developments in hate crime legislation. This variable may show more consistent results in future research.

Figure 63

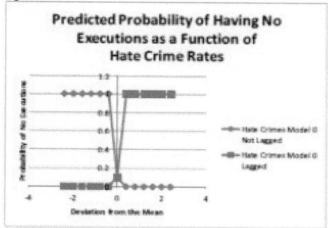

Figure 64

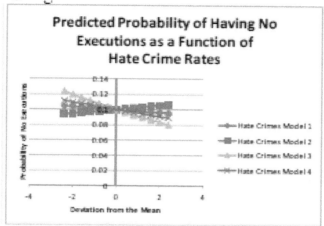

Figure 65

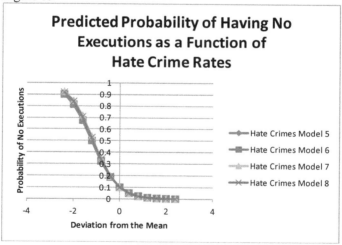

Figures 66, 67, and 68 illustrate the predicted number of executions in states with at least one execution. Models 0 (lagged and non-lagged) and Models 1 – 4 show a positive relationship between hate crimes and executions in states with at least one execution.

However, Model 5 – 8 (Figure 68) shows a negative relationship. Once again, this appears to reflect the relatively new emergence of hate crime legislation and the effect of lagging variables. These results do not support the hypothesis related to hate crime rates and executions.

Figure 66

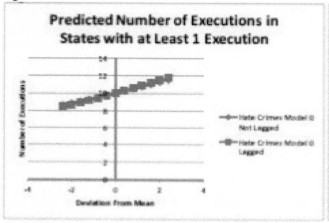

Figure 67

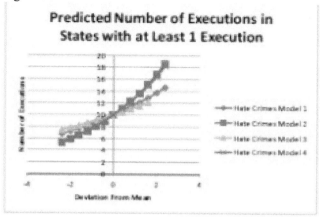

Figure 68

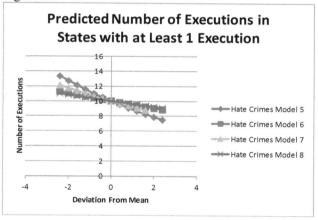

Figures 60, 70, and 71 show the predicted number of executions as a function of hate crime rates. The lagged and non-lagged model 0 shows almost an opposite relationship between hate crime rates an executions, while Models 1 – 4 show a positive relationship. Models 5 – 8 show executions peaking right around the mean, and then decreasing as they move away from the mean. Once again, these results do not support the previous hypothesis.

Figure 69

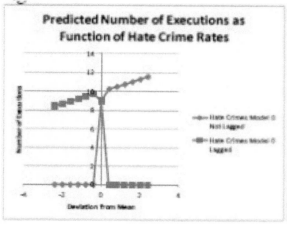

Figure 70

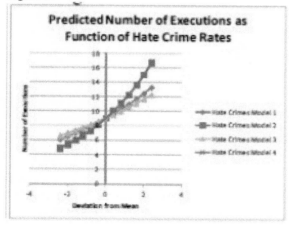

Figure 71

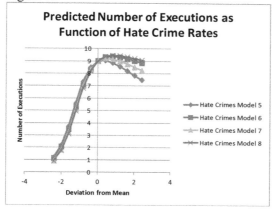

Exonerations and the Death Penalty

Figures 72, 73, and 74 illustrate the predicted probability of having no executions as a function of exonerations. Model 0 (lagged and non-lagged) and Models 1 – 4 show the predicted negative relationship between exonerations and the predicted probability of having no executions, while the results of Models 5 – 8 show the opposite relationship. It is important to take into consideration that the number of executions may increase as the number of exonerations increase. Both executions and exonerations are part of the same process – namely, the appeals process. Executions are going to increase as more inmates exhaust their appeals, but the appeals process allows for more inmates to potentially prove their innocence in a court of law. Also, by lagging the variables, models 5 – 8 take into account the time it takes for the news of exoneration to have an impact on legislation and/or death penalty juries.

Figure 72

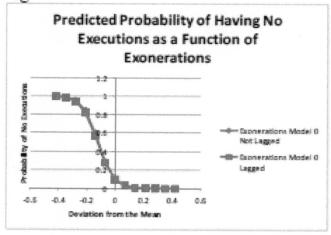

Figure 73

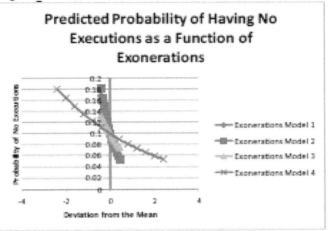

Figure 74

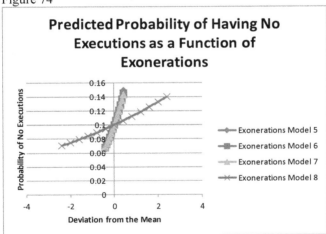

Figures 75, 76 and 77 illustrate the predicted number of executions in states with at least one execution. The results in these figures are less consistent across models. This may be due to the issue of timing, as noted above, and of the more direct relationship of exoneration and executions to the death penalty process.

Figure 75

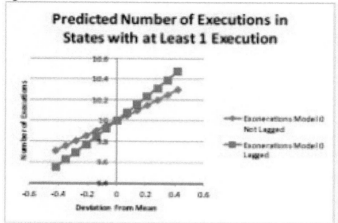

Figure 76

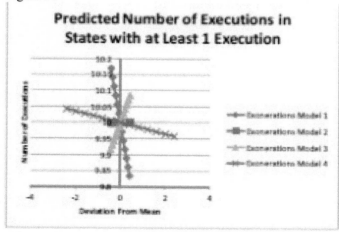

Figure 77

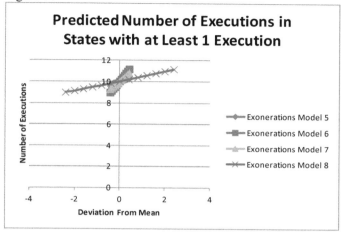

Finally, Figures 78, 79, and 80 show the predicted number of executions as a function of exonerations. Except for Model 5, there appears to be a fairly consistent positive relationship between exonerations and executions. As noted previously, this variable is more closely associated with the capital punishment process than the other variables analyzed here. In order to have exoneration, there needs to be someone sentenced to death. With each new death sentence, the probability of an innocent person being convicted increases.

Figure 78

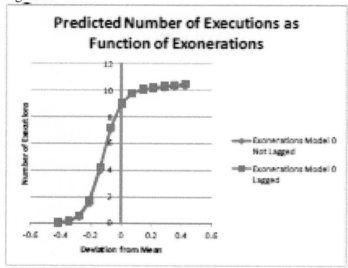

Figure 79

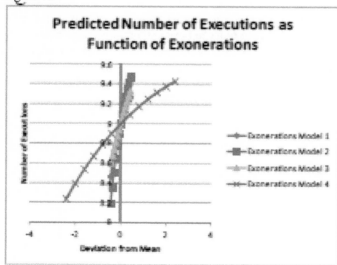

Figure 80

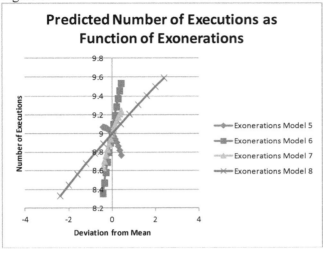

Politics and the Death Penalty

As noted in Figures 81 and 82, the relationship between the death penalty and politics is not clear or consistent. Figure 6 shows the predicted probability of having executions as a function of politics for Model 0, not lagged and lagged. The data from the model that was not lagged shows a more pronounced slope than the lagged model. However, in Figure 7, the relationship between politics and executions is mixed. Model 1 shows a steady decrease as the percentage of Republicans in state legislature increase, while Model 3 shows a positive relationship.

Figure 81

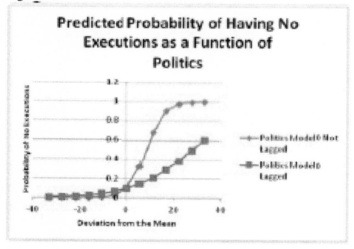

Figure 82

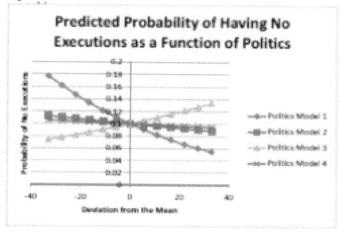

The lagged models resulted in a consistent negative relationship between politics and executions, as shown by the steep slope in Figure 83. As noted previously, this negative relationship may be the result of Southern Democrats' support for law and order policies. These figures illustrate the mixed relationship between politics and executions.

198

198   *Appendices*

Figure 83

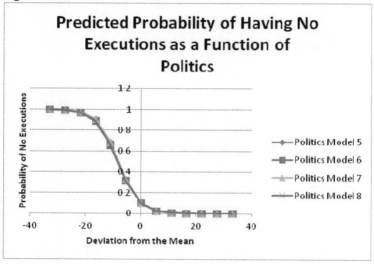

Figures 84, 85, and 86 show the relationship between the predicted number of executions in states with at least 1 execution. Again, the relationship is mixed in Models 0, not lagged and lagged (as illustrated in Figure 84). Figures 85 and 86 show a more consistent relationship among the lagged and not lagged models.

Figure 84

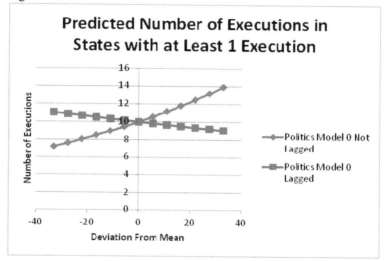

However, Models 1-4 have a positive relationship between politics and the predicted number of executions in states with at least 1 execution (Figure 85), while Models 5-8 shows a negative relationship (Figure 86).

Figure 85

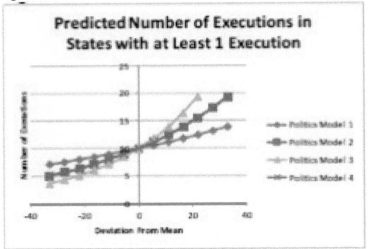

Figure 86

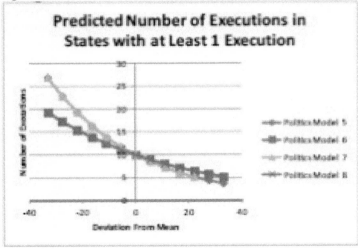

Figures 87, 88, and 89 represent the predicted number of executions as a function of politics. In Figures 12 and 14, the predicted number of executions decreases as values deviate from the mean. Figure 13, however, shows a gradual increase. Interestingly, the slopes on Figure 13 and in Figure 14 are similar within the graphs, but comparing the two graphs demonstrates the lack of consistency with regards to the relationship between executions and politics.

Figure 87

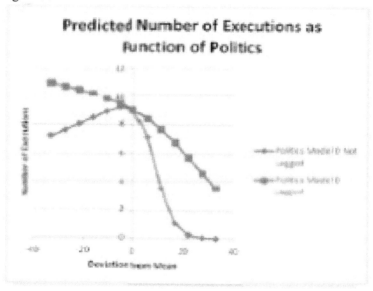

Figure 88

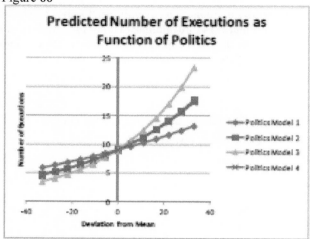

Figure 89

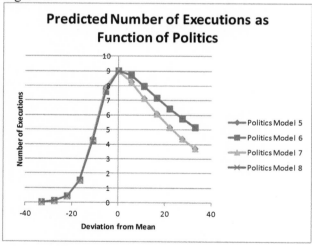

Education and the Death Penalty

Figures 90, 91, and 92 show the predicted probability of having no executions as a function of education. As is the case with politics, the relationship between education and executions is not consistent in the present analysis. Figure 90 shows a positive relationship between executions and the probability of having no executions, which supports the hypothesis noted previously.

Figure 90

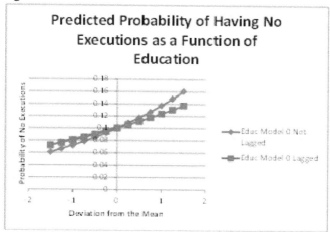

However, Figure 91 shows only a slight increase in Models 1, 2, and 4, while Model 3 shows a notable decrease. Figure 92 demonstrates the negative relationship between education and the noted predicted probability. As noted previously, the addition of education in these models is important as it is part of the socioeconomic status measurement of each state.

Figure 91

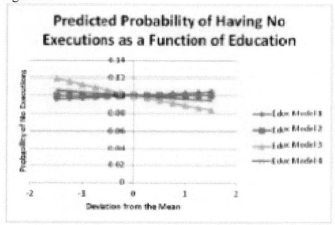

Figure 92

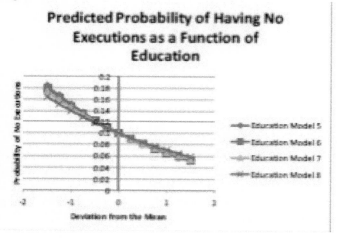

Figures 93, 94, and 95 show the predicted number of executions in states with at least one execution. Again, the relationship between executions and education is mixed. Figure 93 shows a positive relationship, while Figure 94 and 95 do not present as clear of a picture.

It appears from these to figures that removing region from the models creates some consistency (as show by Models 2 and 4 in Figure 94 and Models 6 and 8 in Figure 95).

Figure 93

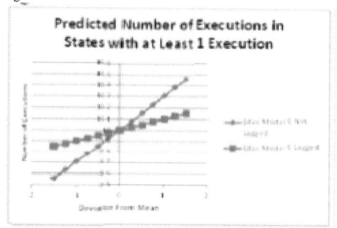

Figure 94

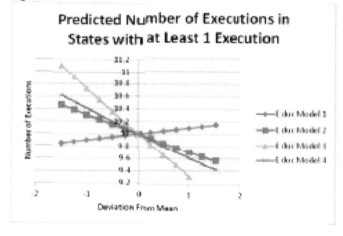

Figure 95

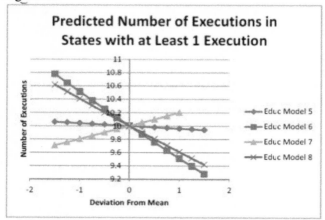

Figures 96, 97, and 98 show the predicted number of executions as a function of education. Once again, the relationship is not consistent across models. In the Model 0 results (both not lagged and lagged), there is a decrease in executions as the education of a state increases. However, in Figure 97, there is a decreasing slope in Models 1, 2, and 4, but an increasing slope in Model 3. Figure 98 shows a consistent relatively minimal increase across the lagged models. Taken together, these figures illustrate the complexity of education and the death penalty.

Figure 96

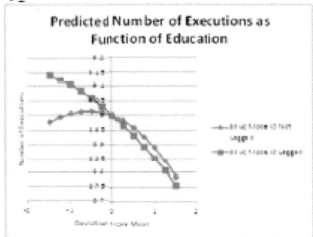

Figure 97

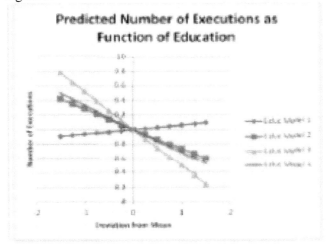

Figure 98

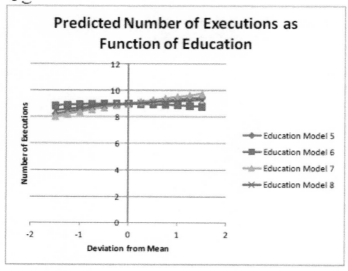

Inequality and the Death Penalty

Figures 99, 100, and 101 illustrate the predicted probability of having no executions as a function of inequality rates. Taking the figures separately, the slopes are consistent within each graph, with Figures 24 and 26 having a negative slope and Figure 25 having a positive slope. The results in Figures 24 and 26 are as predicted and supports the hypothesis related to inequality and the death penalty. However, Figure 25 refutes the hypothesis.

Figure 99

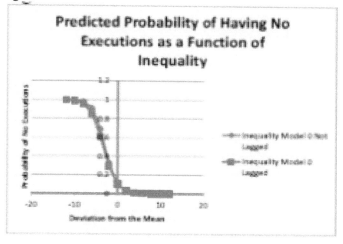

Figure 100

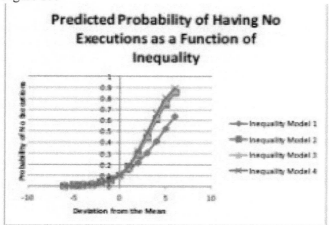

Figure 101

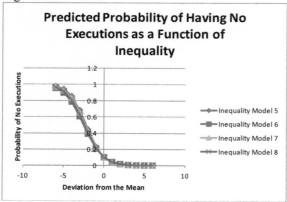

Figures 102, 103, and 104 show the predicted number of executions in states with at least one execution. Once again, the results are mixed. As predicted, there is a positive slope in Model 0 (lagged and not lagged) and in Model 1 and 2. However, the remaining models refute the hypothesis that an increase in inequality rates result in an increase in executions.

Figure 102

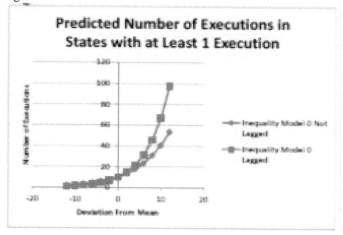

Figure 103

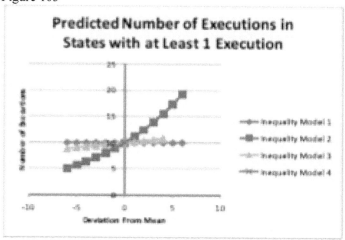

Interestingly the slope is almost exactly the same in the models shown in Figure 29. Thus, the lagging of variables seems to create a more consistent outcome than the non-lagged models.

Figure 104

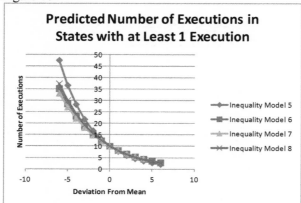

Figures 105, 106, and 107 illustrate the predicted number of executions as a function of inequality rates. Figures 106 and 107 shows more consistency than the previous graphs, but they are still markedly different than Figure 105. These findings refute the hypothesis related to inequality rates and executions.

Figure 105

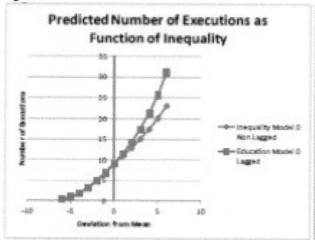

Figure 106

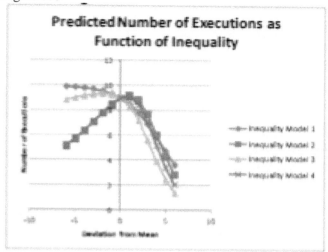

Figure 107

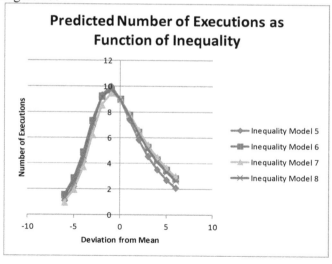

Race and the Death Penalty

Figures 108 and 109 demonstrate the predicted probability of having no executions as a function of the percentage of the population that is Black. These show a consistent finding that the probability of having no executions decreases as the percentage of the population that is Black increases. These results support the hypothesis related to race.

Figure 108

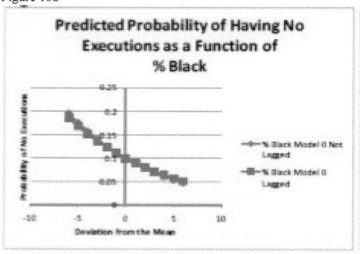

Figure 109

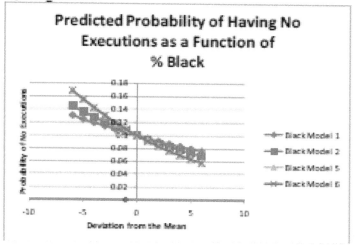

Figures 110 and 111 show the predicted number of executions in states with at least one execution. The results for the models are mixed. Figure 35 shows that the lagged model has a steeper slope than the non-lagged, while region seems to change the direction of the correlation as shown in Figure 111. The relationship appears to be negative when controlling for region (Models 1 and 5) and positive when not controlling for region (Models 2 and 6).

Figure 110

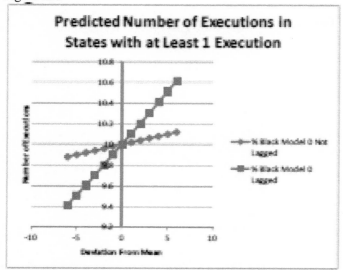

Figure 111

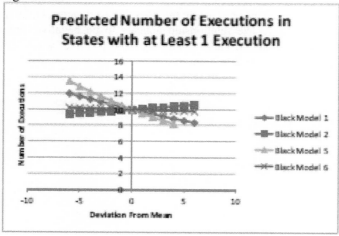

Figures 112 and 113 illustrate the predicted number of executions as a function of the percentage of the population that is Black. Consistent with Figures 110 and 111, Figures 112 and 113 show a positive relationship in Model 0 (lagged and non-lagged) and in Models 2 and 4. These results suggest that region does have an influence on the results and the relationship between race and executions.

Figure 112

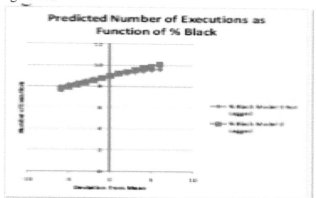

Figure 113

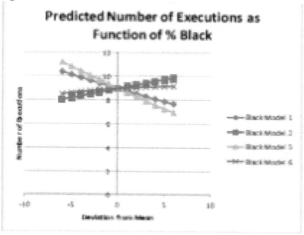

Figures 114, 115, and 116 illustrate the predicted probability of having no executions as a function of percentage of the population that is Black + percentage of the population that is Hispanic. Model 0 (lagged and non-lagged) and Models 3 and 4 shows the predicted negative relationship between race and executions. Models 7 and 8, however, show a positive relationship.

Figure 114

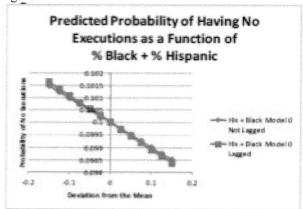

Figure 115

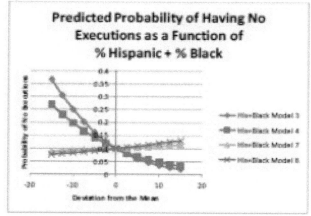

Figures 116 and 117 illustrate the predicted number of executions in states with at least one execution. The lagged and non-lagged models follow the same positive slope. However, Models 3, 4, 7, and 8 are not consistent. This may be the result of the complexity of race in America generally, and within the criminal justice system specifically. These results refute the hypothesis related to race.

Figure 116

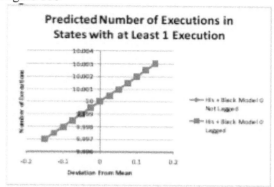

Figure 117

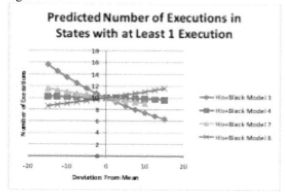

Figures 118 and 119 shows the predicted number of executions as a function of the percentage of the population that is Black plus the percentage of the population that is Hispanic. Once again Model 0 (lagged and non-lagged) have the same slope, while Model 3, 4, 7, and 8 show differing slopes. Region appears to be a significant factor in these models, since the models controlling for region have a negative slope, while those not controlling for region has a positive slope. Therefore, region seems to be more significant and influential than race in these analyses.

Figure 118

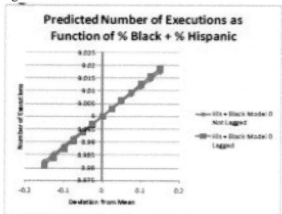

Figure 119

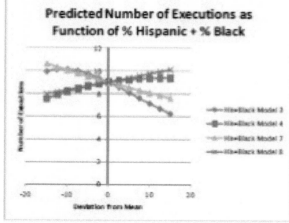

Evangelicals and the Death Penalty

Figures 120, 121, and 122 illustrate the predicted probability of having no executions as a function of Evangelicals. These graphs show some consistency across models when it comes to the influence of Evangelicals. The negative slope suggest that as the percentage of Evangelicals increase, the probability of having no executions decreases, which supports the hypothesis related to capital punishment and Evangelicals.

Figure 120

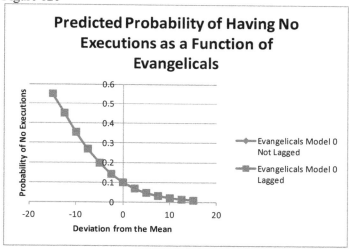

Figure 121

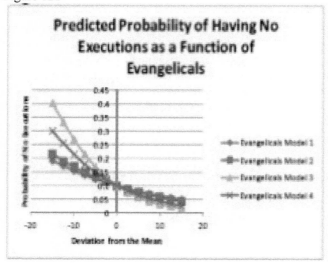

Figure 122

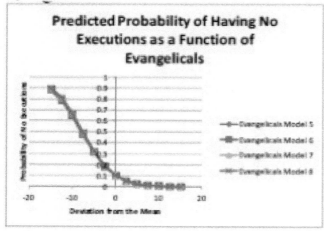

Figures 123, 124, and 125 illustrate the predicted number of executions in states with at least one execution. As with the previous discussion, the results are relatively consistent across models. There is a positive relationship between Evangelicals and executions. As Tables 6 and 7 showed, this relationship is not only consistent, but significant across models.

Figure 123

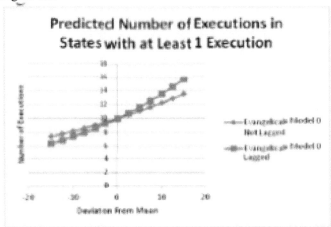

Figure 124

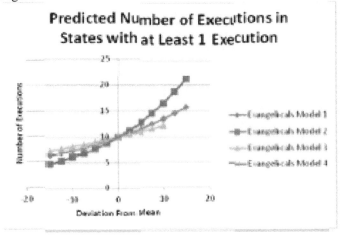

Figure 125

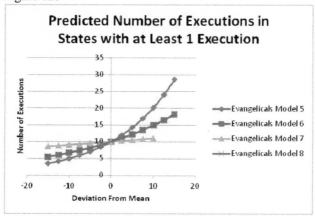

Figures 126, 127, and 128 show the predicted number of executions as a function of Evangelicals. As predicted, an increase in the percentage of Evangelicals results in an increase in the predicted number of executions across models.

Figure 126

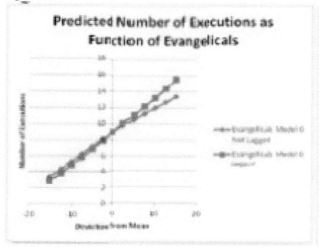

Figure 127

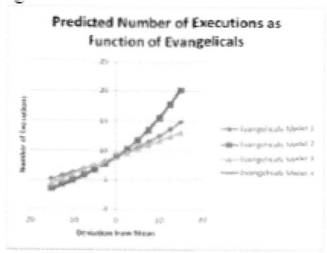

Figure 128

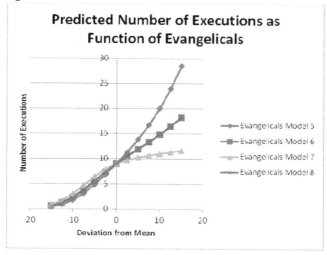

Homicide Rates and the Death Penalty

Figures 129, 130 and 131 illustrate the predicted probability of having no executions as a function of homicide rates. The results are consistent across models, but the relationship is not as predicted. This data show that an increase in homicide rates result in a decreased probability of having no executions. This is not surprising given that homicide rates tended to have a significant correlation with the adoption and not necessarily the implementation of the death penalty.

Figure 129

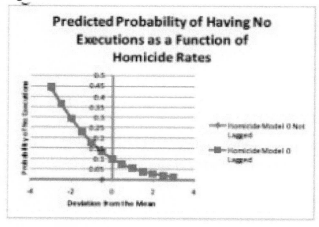

Figure 130

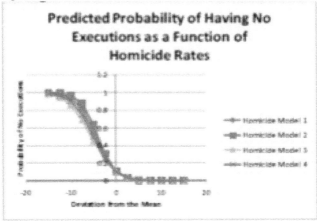

Figure 131

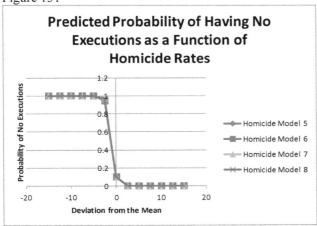

Figures 132, 133, and 134 illustrate the predicted number of executions in states with at least one execution. Once again, the results across models are similar in slope, but contrary to what was hypothesized previously. The negative correlation suggests that homicide rates are not necessarily the driving force behind executions.

Thus the other variables in this dissertation appear to have a more significant influence.

Figure 132

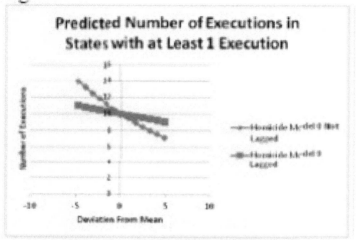

Figure 133

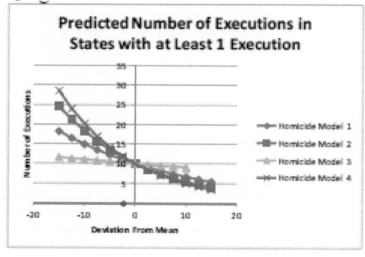

Figure 134

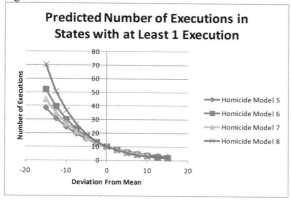

Figures 135, 136, and 137 show the predicted number of executions as a function of homicide rates. Interestingly, executions appear to reach a peak at the mean, then decrease as the deviation from the mean increases across all the models. This again suggests that crime is not the driving force behind the differences in the number of executions across states, thus supporting social control and social dominance theories.

Figure 135

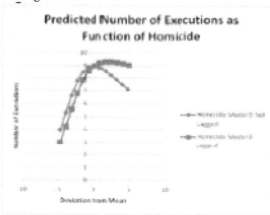

Figure 136

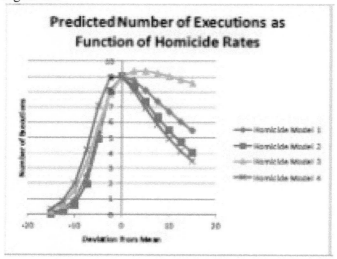

Figure 137

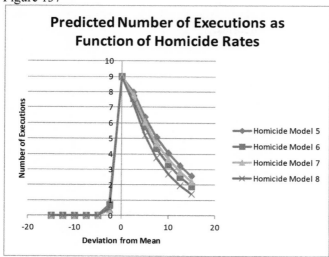

Hate Crime Rates and the Death Penalty

Figures 138, 139, and 140 illustrate the predicted probability of having no executions as a function of hate crime rates. The lagged and non-lagged models in Figure 138 shows a completely opposite relationship between executions and hate crime rates. Models 1 – 4 in Figure 139 also show mixed results, while Figure 140 shows that Models 5 – 8 are more consistent. This may be due to two factors. First, hate crimes are prosecuted in a subjective manner (i.e. one prosecutor may files hate crime charges in one case, while another with a similar set of facts may not). Second, the lagging of variables appears to have helped create more consistency, which in turn may be the result of the relatively recent developments in hate crime legislation. This variable may show more consistent results in future research.

Figure 138

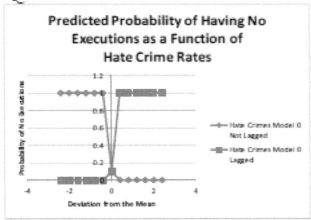

Figure 139

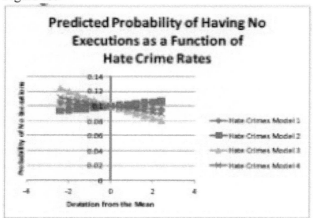

Figure 140

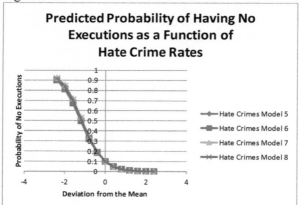

Figures 141, 142, and 143 illustrate the predicted number of executions in states with at least one execution. Models 0 (lagged and non-lagged) and Models 1 – 4 show a positive relationship between hate crimes and executions in states with at least one execution. However, Model 5 – 8 (Figure 143) shows a negative relationship. Once again, this appears to reflect the relatively new emergence of hate crime legislation and the effect of lagging variables. These results do not support the hypothesis related to hate crime rates and executions.

Figure 141

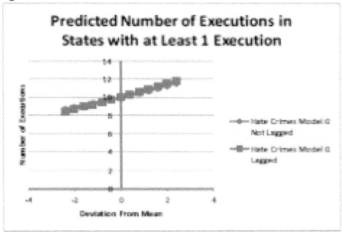

Figure 142

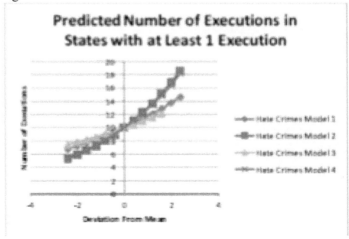

Figure 143

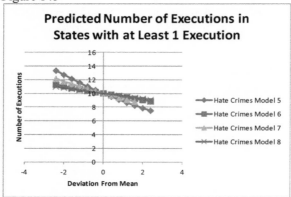

Figures 141, 142, and 143 show the predicted number of executions as a function of hate crime rates. The lagged and non-lagged model 0 shows almost an opposite relationship between hate crime rates an executions, while Models 1 – 4 show a positive relationship. Models 5 – 8 show executions peaking right around the mean, and then decreasing as they move away from the mean. Once again, these results do not support the previous hypothesis.

Figure 144

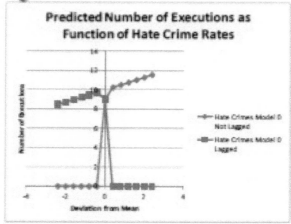

Figure 145

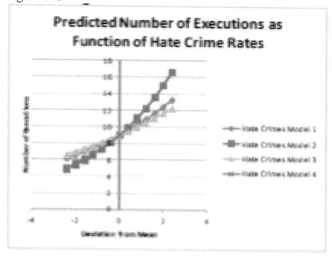

Figure 146

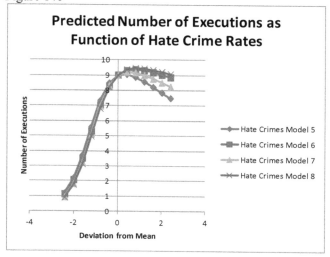

Exonerations and the Death Penalty

Figures 147, 148, and 149 illustrate the predicted probability of having no executions as a function of exonerations. Model 0 (lagged and non-lagged) and Models 1 – 4 show the predicted negative relationship between exonerations and the predicted probability of having no executions, while the results of Models 5 – 8 show the opposite relationship. It is important to take into consideration that the number of executions may increase as the number of exonerations increase. Both executions and exonerations are part of the same process – namely, the appeals process. Executions are going to increase as more inmates exhaust their appeals, but the appeals process allows for more inmates to potentially prove their innocence in a court of law. Also, by lagging the variables, models 5 – 8 take into account the time it takes for the news of exoneration to have an impact on legislation and/or death penalty juries.

Figure 147

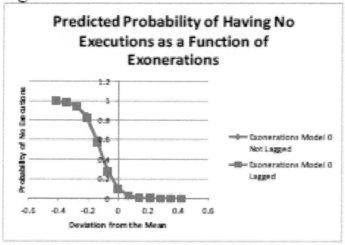

Figure 148

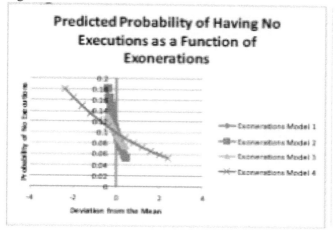

Figure 149

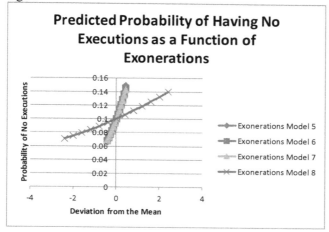

Figures 150, 151, and 152 illustrate the predicted number of executions in states with at least one execution. The results in these figures are less consistent across models. This may be due to the issue of timing, as noted above, and of the more direct relationship of exoneration and executions to the death penalty process.

Figure 150

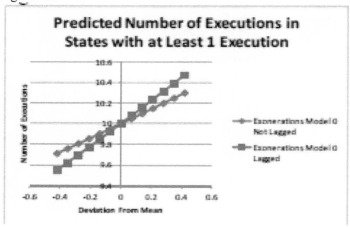

Figure 151

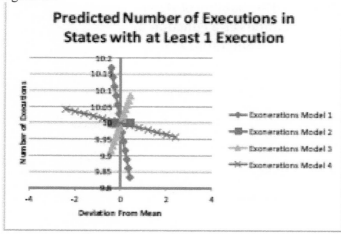

Figure 152

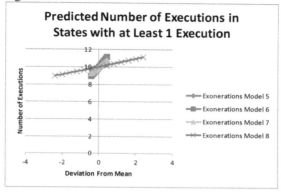

Finally, Figures 153, 154, and 155 show the predicted number of executions as a function of exonerations. Except for Model 5, there appears to be a fairly consistent positive relationship between exonerations and executions. As noted previously, this variable is more closely associated with the capital punishment process than the other variables analyzed here. In order to have exoneration, there needs to be someone sentenced to death; with each new death sentence, the probability of an innocent person being convicted increases.

Figure 153

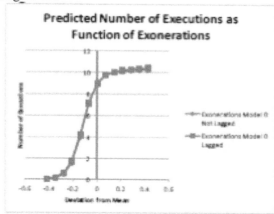

Figure 154

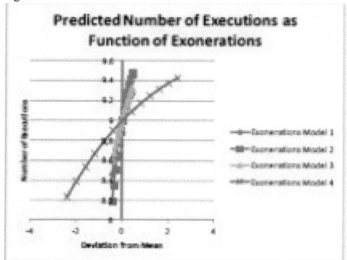

Figure 155

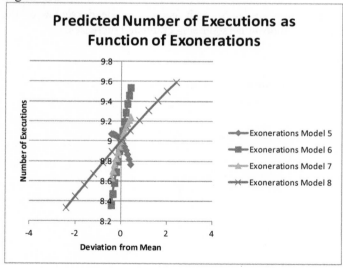

Bibliography

Acker, James R., Bohm, Robert M., and Lanier, Charles S. (2003). *America's Experiment with Capital Punishment: Reflections on the Past, Present, and Future of the Ultimate Penal Sanction.* Durham, N.C.: Carolina Academic Press.

Adams, Jessica. (2007). *Wounds of Returning: Race, Memory, and Property on the Postslavery Plantation.* Chapel Hill, N.C.: The University of North Carolina Press.

Alper, Ty. (2006). "Lethal Incompetence: Lethal Injection Litigation is Exposing More than Tortuous Executions." *The Champion.* Retrieved February 25, 2008 from http://www.law.berkeley.edu/clinics/dpclinic/LethalInjection/Public/Articl es/Journals/alper.champion.pdf.

American Bar Association, Death Penalty Moratorium Implementation Project. (2007). "State Death Penalty Assessments: Key Findings." Retrieved February 19, 2008 from http://www.abanet.org/moratorium/assessmentproject/keyfindings.doc.

American Bar Association, Death Penalty Moratorium Implementation Project. (2007a). "Death Penalty Moratorium Implementation Project. Assessment of Capital Jurisdictions: Frequently Asked Questions." Retrieved March 28, 2008 from http://www.abanet.org/moratorium/assessmentproject/faq.doc.

American Bar Association, Juvenile Justice Center. (2004). "Cruel and Unusual Punishment: The Juvenile Death Penalty - Adolescence, Brain Development and Legal Culpability." Retrieved February 15, 2008 from http://www.abanet.org/crimjust/juvjus/Adolescence.pdf.

American Bar Association, Section of Individual Rights and Responsibilities. (2001). "Death without Justice: A Guide for Examining the

Administration of the Death Penalty in the United States." Retrieved October 5, 2007 from http://www.abanet.org/irr/finaljune28.pdf.

American Bar Association. (2003). "American Bar Association Section of Individual Rights and Responsibilities, Toward Greater Awareness: The American Bar Association Call for a Moratorium on Executions Gains Ground." Retrieved November 25, 2007 from http://www.abanet.org/irr/publications/Aug03Moratoriumreport.html.

American Civil Liberties Union. (2004). "The Death Penalty Debate." Retrieved February 15, 2008 from https://www.aclu.org/capital/general/10527pub20040319.html.

American College of Physicians. (2005). "Ethics Manual: Fifth Edition." Retrieved November 24, 2007 from http://www.acponline.org/ethics/ethicman5th.htm.

American Medical Association (AMA). (2003). "D-140.979 Moratorium on the Imposition of the Death Penalty." Retrieved November 24, 2007 from http://www.ama-assn.org/apps/pf_new/pf_online? f_n=browse &doc=policyfiles/DIR/D-140.979.HTM.

American Medical Association (AMA). (2007). "Pending Federal Executions." Retrieved November 24, 2007 from http://www.amaassn.org/apps/pf_new/pf_online?f_n=browse&doc=policy files/DIR/D-140.980.HTM&&s_t=&st_p=&nth=1&prev_ pol=policyfiles/DIR/D-135.999.HTM&nxt_pol=policyfiles/DIR/D-140.969.HTM&.

American Nurses Association (ANA). (1994). "Position Statement: Nurses' Participation in Capital Punishment." Retrieved November 24, 2007 from http://www.nursingworld.org/MainMenuCategories/HealthcareandPolicyIss ues/ANAPositionStatements/EthicsandHumanRights.aspx.

American Public Health Association (APHA). (2001). "Participation of Health Professionals in Capital Punishment." Retrieved November 24, 2007 from http://www.apha.org/advocacy/policy/policysearch/default.htm?id=264.

American Society of Anesthesiologists. (2006). "Statement on Physician Nonparticipation in Legally Authorized Executions." Retrieved November 24, 2007 from http://www.asahq.org/publicationsAndServices/standards/41.pdf.

Amnesty International (2002). "The Abolition Movement: A Brief History." Retrieved November 24, 2007 from http://www.amnestyusa.org/abolish/event2/history.html.

Amnesty International. (2007). "Execution by Lethal Injection: A Quarter Century of State Poisoning." Retrieved March 3, 2008 from http://www.amnestyusa.org/document.php?lang=e&id=ENGACT5000720 07.

Amnesty International. (2008). "Recent Death Penalty Trends." Retrieved March 5, 2008 from http://www.amnestyusa.org/abolish/factsheets/FactSheets.doc.

Archer, Dane, Gartner, Rosemary, and Beittel, Marc. (1983). "Homicide and the Death Penalty: A Cross-National Test of a Deterrence Hypothesis." *The Journal of Criminal Law and Criminology*. 74:3. pp. 991-1013.

Atkins v. Virginia (536 U.S. 304 (2002). Retrieved November 24, 2007 from http://supct.law.cornell.edu/supct/html/00-8452.ZS.html.

Atkins, David C. and Robert J. Gallop. (2007). "Rethinking How Family Researchers Model In frequent Outcomes: A Tutorial on Count Regression and Zero-Inflated Models." *Journal of Family Psychology*. 21:4. pp. 726-735.

Atwell, Mary Welek. (2004). *Evolving Standards of Decency: Popular Culture and Capital Punishment*. New York: P. Lang.

Bailey, William C. (1974). "Murder and the Death Penalty." *The Journal of Criminal Law and Criminology*. 65:3. pp. 416-423.

Bailey, William C. (1998). "Deterrence, Brutalization, and the Death Penalty: Another Examination of Oklahoma's Return to Capital Punishment." *Criminology*. 36:4. pp. 711-733.

Bailey, William C. and Ruth D. Peterson, (1994). "Murder, Capital Punishment, and Deterrence: A Review of the Evidence and an Examination of Police Killings." *Journal of Social Issues*. 50:2. pp. 53-75.

Baldus, David C., George Woodworth, and Charles A. Pulaski, Jr. (1990). *Equal Justice and the Death Penalty: A Legal and Empirical Analysis*. Boston: Northeastern University Press; University Press of New England.

Baldus, David C., George Woodworth, David Zuckerman, Neil Alan Weiner, and Barbara Broffitt. (1998). "Racial Discrimination and the Death Penalty in the Post-Furman Era: An Empirical and Legal Overview, with Recent Findings from Philadelphia." *Cornell Law Review*. 83. pp. 1638-1771.

Banner, Stuart. (2002). *The Death Penalty: An American History*. Cambridge, Mass.: Harvard University Press.

Barrows, Samuel J. (1907). "Legislative Tendencies as to Capital Punishment."
   Annals of the American Academy of Political and Social Science. 29. pp.
   178-181.

Bassett, Laura. (April 25, 2012). "Connecticut Repeals Death Penalty."
   Huffington Post. Retrieved June 25, 2012 from
   http://www.huffingtonpost.com/2012/04/25/connecticut-repeals-death-
   penalty_n_1453331.html.

Baumer, Eric P., Messner, Steven F., and Rosenfeld, Richard. (2003).
   "Explaining Spatial Variation in Support for Capital Punishment: A
   Multilevel Analysis." *The American Journal of Sociology.* 108:4 pp. 844-
   875.

Baumgartner, Frank R., Suzanna L. DeBoef, and Amber E. Boydstun. (2008).
   The Decline of the Death Penalty and the Discovery of Innocence.
   Cambridge, New York, Melbourne, Madrid, Cape Town, Singapore, Sao
   Paulo, Delhi: Cambridge University Press.

Baze v. Rees (No. 07-5439) 217 S. W. 3d 207 (2008). Retrieved June 22, 2009
   from http://www.law.cornell.edu/supct/html/07-5439.ZO.html.

Beauchamp, T. & Childress, J. (2001) *Principles of Biomedical Ethics, 5th Ed.*
   Oxford University Press.

Bedau, Hugo Adam. (2004). *Killing as Punishment: Reflections on the Death
   Penalty in America.* Boston: Northeastern University Press.

Bennett, Colin J. and Michael Howlett. (1992). "The Lessons of Learning:
   Reconciling Theories of Policy Learning and Policy Change." *Policy
   Sciences.* 25:3. pp. 275-294 Retrieved May 14, 2009 from
   http://www.jstor.org/stable/4532260.

Berry, Frances Stokes, and William D. Berry. 1990. "State Lottery Adoptions
   as Policy Innovations: An Event History Analysis." *American Political
   Science Review.* 84: 395-416.

Beschle, Donald L. (1997). "What's Guilt (or Deterrence) Got to do With It?
   The Death Penalty, Ritual and Mimetic Violence." *William and Mary Law
   Review,* Jan, v. 38, n. 2, pg. 487-538.

Bessler, John D. (1997). *Death in the Dark: Midnight Executions in America.*
   Boston: Northeastern University Press.

Blau, Judith R. and Peter M. Blau . (1982). "The Cost of Inequality:
   Metropolitan Structure and Violent Crime." *American Sociological
   Review.* 47:1. pp. 114-129. Retrieved May 19, 2009 from
   http://www.jstor.org/stable/2095046.

Blomberg, Thomas G. and Lucken, Karol. (2000). *American Penology: A History of Control*. Hawthorne, NY: Aldine Transaction.

Blume, John H., Theodore Eisenberg, and Sheri Lynn Johnson. (1998). "Post-McCleskey Racial Discrimination Claims in Capital Cases." *Cornell Law Review*. 83:1772.

Bobo, Lawrence and Ryan A. Smith. (1998). "From Jim, Crow Racism to Laissez Faire Racism: The Transformation of Racial Attitudes." Pp. 182-220 in *Beyond Pluralism: The Conception of Groups and Group Identities in America*. Edited by Wendy F. Katkin, Ned Landsman, and Andrea Tyree. Urbana, IL: University of Illinois Press.

Bowers, William J. (1996). "The Capital Jury: Is It Tilted toward Death?" *Judicature*. 79: pp. 220-223.

Bowers, William. (1993). "Research Note: Capital Punishment and Contemporary Values: People's Misgivings and the Court's Misperceptions" *Law & Society Review*. 27:1. pp. 157-176.

Bright, Stephen B. (1994). "Counsel for the Poor: The Death Sentence Not for the Worst Crime but for the Worst Lawyer." *The Yale Law Journal*. 103:7. pp. 1835-1883.

Bright, Stephen B. (1995). "Discrimination, Death and Denial: The Tolerance of Racial Discrimination in Infliction of the Death Penalty." *Santa Clara Law Review*. 35. pp. 433-483.

Bright, Stephen B. and Patrick J. Keenan. (1995). "Judges and the Politics of Death: Deciding Between the Bill of Rights and the Next Election in Capital Cases." *Boston University Law Review*. 75:760. pp. 759-836.

Bruderl, Josef. (2005). "Panel Data Analysis." Retrieved December 14, 2008 from http://www.sowi.uni-mannheim.de/lehrstuehle/lessm/veranst/Panelanalyse.pdf.

Bulter, Brooke M. and Moran, Gary. (2002). "The Role of Death Qualification in Venirepersons' Evaluations of Aggravating and Mitigating Circumstances in Capital Trials." *Law and Human Behavior*. 26:2. pp. 175-184.

Burnstein, Paul. (2003). "The Impact of Public Opinion on Public Policy: A Review and an Agenda." *Political Research Quarterly*. 56:1. pp. 29-40.

Bye, Raymond. (1926). "Recent History and Present Status of Capital Punishment in the United States." *Journal of the American Institute of Criminal Law and Criminology*. 17:2. pp. 234-245.

Caroll, Leo and Pamela Irving Jackson. (1983). "Inequality, Opportunity, and Crime Rates in Central Cities." *Criminology*. 21:2. pp. 178-194. Retrieved May 19, 2009 from http://dx.doi.org/10.1111/j.1745-9125.1983.tb00257.x.

Carr, James M. (1987). "At Witt's End: The Continuing Quandary of Jury Selection in Capital Cases." *Stanford Law Review*. 39:2. pp. 427-460.

Chambliss, William J. and R. Seidman. (1980). *Law, Order, and Power*. Reading, PA: Addison-Wesley.

Clement, Douglas (2002). "A Punishing Debate." *The Region*, June, v. 16, pp. 12-15.

Cloninger, Dale O. (1992). "Capital Punishment and Deterrence: A Portfolio Approach." *Applied Economics*, June, v. 24, n. 6, pp. 635-645.

Cloninger, Dale O. and Roberto Marchesini. (2001). "Execution and Deterrence: A Quasi-Controlled Group Experiment." *Applied Economics*, April, v. 33, i. 5, pp. 569-576.

Cochran, John K. and Mitchell B, Chamlin. (2006). "The Enduring Racial Divide in Death Penalty Support." *Journal of Criminal Justice*. 34: 1. pp. 85-99.

Cohen, Stanley. (2003). *The Wrong Men: America's Epidemic of Wrongful Death Row Convictions*. New York: Barnes and Noble.

Coker v. Georgia 433 U.S. 584 (1977). Retrieved November 24, 2007 from http://supct.law.cornell.edu/supct/search/display.html?terms=Coker%20v.%20Georgia&url=/supct/html/historics/USSC_CR_0433_0584_ZO.html.

Cook, Kerry Max. (2007). *Chasing Justice: My Story of Freeing Myself After Two Decades on Death Row for a Crime I Didn't Commit*. New York: HarperCollins.

Cortese, Anthony. (2006). "The Death Penalty: A Case of Institutional Racism." *Paper presented at the annual meeting of the American Sociological Association, Montreal Convention Center, Montreal, Quebec, Canada*, Aug 10, 2006. Retrieved August 19, 2008 from http://www.allacademic.com/meta/p96435_index.html.

Coyne, Randall and Entzeroth, Lyn. (2001). *Capital Punishment and the Judicial Process*. Durham, NC: Carolina Academic Press.

Cutler, J.E. (1907). "Capital Punishment and Lynching." *Annals of the American Academy of Political and Social Science*. 29. pp. 182-185.

Davis, Ada J. (1930). "The Evolution of the Institution of Mothers' Pensions in the United States." *American Journal of Sociology*. 35. pp. 573-82.

Death Penalty Information Center (DPIC). (2014). "Facts about the Death Penalty." Retrieved April 2, 2014 from http://www.deathpenaltyinfo.org/documents/FactSheet.pdf.

Death Penalty Information Center (DPIC). (2014a). "Number of Executions by State and Region Since 1976." Retrieved April 6, 2014 from http://www.deathpenaltyinfo.org/state_by_state.

Death Penalty Information Center (DPIC). (2014b). "Innocence: List of Those Freed From Death Row." Retrieved April 6, 2014 from http://www.deathpenaltyinfo.org/innocence-list-those-freed-death-row?scid=6&did=110.

Death Penalty Information Center (DPIC). (2014c). "Death Row Inmates by State." Retrieved April 6, 2014 from http://www.deathpenaltyinfo.org/death-row-inmates-state-and-size-death-row-year.

Death Penalty Information Center (DPIC). (2014c). "Number of Executions by State and Region Since 1976." Retrieved April 6, 2014 from http://www.deathpenaltyinfo.org/number-executions-state-and-region-1976.

Death Penalty Information Center (DPIC). (2012). "Poll Shows Growing Support for Alternatives to the Death Penalty; Capital Punishment Ranked Lowest Among Budget Priorities." Retrieved April 24, 2012 from http://www.deathpenaltyinfo.org/pollresults.

Death Penalty Information Center (DPIC). (2011). "State by State Database." Retrieved June 26, 2012 from http://www.deathpenaltyinfo.org/state_by_state.

Death Penalty Information Center (DPIC). (2011a). "Facts About the Death Penalty." Retrieved September 16, 2011 from http://www.deathpenaltyinfo.org/documents/FactSheet.pdf.

Death Penalty Information Center (DPIC). (2008a). "Arbitrariness." Retrieved March 7, 2008 from http://www.deathpenaltyinfo.org/article.php?did=1328.

Death Penalty Information Center (DPIC). (2007a). "Mental Retardation and the Death Penalty." Retrieved November 24, 2007 from http://www.deathpenaltyinfo.org/article.php?scid=28&did=176.

Death Penalty Information Center (DPIC). (2007b). "Illinois Death Row Inmates Granted Commutation by Governor George Ryan on January 12, 2003." Retrieved December 2, 2007 from http://www.deathpenaltyinfo.org/article.php?scid=13&did=485.

Deets, Lee Emerson. (1948). "Changes in Capital Punishment Policy since 1939." *Journal of Criminal Law and Criminology*. 38:6. pp. 584-594.

Department of Justice, Office of Justice Programs, Bureau of Justice Statistics. (2006). "Capital offenses by State, 2006." Retrieved March 28, 2008 from http://www.ojp.usdoj.gov/bjs/pub/html/cp/2006/tables/cp06st01.htm.

Dieter, Richard C. (1996). "Killing for Votes: The Dangers of Politicizing the Death Penalty Process." Death Penalty Information Center. Retrieved August 19, 2008 from
http://www.deathpenaltyinfo.org/article.php?did=260&scid=.

Dieter, Richard C. (1998). "The Death Penalty in Black and White: Who Lives, Who Dies, Who Decides?" *Death Penalty Information Center*. Retrieved November 22, 2007 from
http://www.deathpenaltyinfo.org/article.php?did=539&scid=.

Dieter, Richard C. (2005). "Blind Justice: Juries Deciding Life and Death with Only Half the Truth." *Death Penalty Information Center*. Retrieved November 12, 2009 from
http://www.deathpenaltyinfo.org/BlindJusticeReport.pdf.

Dieter, Richard C., Esq. (1994). "Millions Misspent: What Politicians Don't Say About the High Costs of the Death Penalty." Retrieved November 2, 2009 from http://www.deathpenaltyinfo.org/node/599.

Dolinko, David. (1986). "Foreword: How to Criticize the Death Penalty." *The Journal of Criminal Law and Criminology*. 77:3. pp. 546-601.

Donohue, John J. and Justin Wolfers. (2005). "Uses and Abuses of Empirical Evidence in the Death Penalty Debate." *Stanford Law Review*. 58:3. pp. 791-845.

Dougherty, Christopher. (2006). *Introduction to Econometrics*. Retrieved December 14, 2008 from
http://www.oup.com/uk/orc/bin/9780199280964/dougherty_chap14.pdf.

Dow, David R. and Dow, Mark. (eds.) (2002). *Machinery of Death: The Reality of America's Death Penalty Regime*. New York: Routledge.

Eckhardt, William. (1991). "Authoritarianism." *Political Psychology*. 12:1. pp. 97-124.

Eisenberg, Theodore, Stephen P. Garvey, and Martin T. Wells. (2001). "Forecasting Life and Death: Juror Race, Religion, and Attitude Toward the Death Penalty." *Journal of Legal Studies*. 30. pp. 277-311.

Elkins, Zachary and Beth Simmons. (2005). "On Waves, Clusters, and Diffusion: A Conceptual Framework." *The Annals of the American*

Academy of Political and Social Science. 598. pp. 33-51. Retrieved May 14, 2009 from http://ann.sagepub.com/cgi/reprint/598/1/33.

Erskine, Hazel. (1970). "The Polls: Capital Punishment." *The Public Opinion Quarterly.* 34:2. pp. 290-307.

Espy, M. Watt and Smykla, John Ortiz. (2000). "Executions is the U.S. 1608-2002: The ESPY File Executions by State." Retrieved November 24, 2007 from http://www.deathpenaltyinfo.org/ESPYstate.pdf.

Fajnzylber, Pablo, Daniel Lederman and Norman Loayza. (2002). "Inequality and Crime." *The Journal of Law and Economics.* 45. Retrieved May 19, 2009 from
http://www.journals.uchicago.edu/doi/full/10.1086/338347?cookieSet=1.

Federal Bureau of Investigation (FBI). (N.D.). "Civil Rights. Hate Crime – Overview." Retrieved April 6, 2014 from
http://www.fbi.gov/about-us/investigate/civilrights/hate_crimes/overview.

Fikes v. Alabama 352 U.S. 191 (1957). Retrieved November 24, 2007 from http://vlex.com/vid/20013199.

Filler, Louis. (1952). "Movements to Abolish the Death Penalty in the United States." *Annals of the American Academy of Political and Social Science.* 284. pp. 124-136.

Fitzgerald, Robert and Ellsworth, Phoebe C. (1984). "Due Process vs. Crime Control: Death Qualification and Jury Attitudes." *Law and Human Behavior.* 8:1/2. pp. 31-51.

Fleming, Annaliese Flynn. (1999). "Louisiana's Newest Capital Crime: The Death Penalty for Child Rape." *The Journal of Criminal Law and Criminology.* 89:2. pp. 717-750.

Fleury-Steiner, Benjamin D., Kerry Dunn and Ruth Fleury-Steiner. (2009). "Governing through Crime as Commonsense Racism: Race, Space, and Death Penalty 'Reform' in Delaware." *Punishment & Society.* 11: 1. pp. 5-24.

Fleury-Steiner, Benjamin. (2004). *Jurors' Stories of Death: How America's Death Penalty Invests in Inequality.* Ann Arbor: University of Michigan Press.

Foley, Michael A. (2003). *Arbitrary and Capricious: The Supreme Court, the Constitution, and the Death Penalty.* Westport, Conn.: Praeger.

Ford v. Wainwright 477 U.S. 399 (1986). Retrieved November 24, 2007 from http://supct.law.cornell.edu/supct/search/display.html?terms=Ford%20v.%20Wainwright&url=/supct/html/historics/USSC_CR_0477_0399_ZO.html.

Franck, Hans Goran (2003). *The Barbaric Punishment: Abolishing the Death Penalty.* The Hague; New York: Martinus Nijhoff Publishers.

Furman v. Georgia 408 U.S. 238 (1972). Retrieved November 24, 2007 from http://caselaw.lp.findlaw.com/scripts/getcase.pl?navby=CASE&court=US &vol=408&page=238.

Galliher, James M. and Galliher, John F. (1997). "Deja Vu All over Again: The Recurring Life and Death of Capital Punishment Legislation in Kansas." *Social Problems.* 44:3. pp. 369-385.

Galliher, James M. and Galliher, John F. (2001). "A 'Commonsense' Theory of Deterrence and the 'Ideology' of Science: The New York State Death Penalty Debate." *The Journal of Criminal Law and Criminology.* 92:1/2. pp. 307-334.

Galliher, John F., Ray, Gregory, and Cook, Brent. (1992). "Abolition and Reinstatement of Capital Punishment During the Progressive Era and Early 20th Century." *The Journal of Criminal Law and Criminology.* 83:3. pp. 538-576.

Gardner, William, Edward P. Mulvey, and Esther Shaw. (1995). "Regression Analyses of Counts and Rates: Poisson, Overdispersed Poisson, and Negative Binomials." *Psychological Bulletin.* 118:3. pp. 392-404.

Garvey, Stephen P. (ed.) (2003). *Beyond Repair? America's Death Penalty.* Durham, NC: Duke University Press.

Gerstein, Richard M. (1960). "A Prosecutor Looks at Capital Punishment." *The Journal of Criminal Law, Criminology, and Police Science.* 51:2. pp. 252-256.

Godfrey v. Georgia 446 U.S. 420 (1980). Retrieved November 24, 2007 from http://supreme.justia.com/us/446/420/.

Goetz, Stephan J. (2005). "Migration and Local Labor Markets." *The Web Book of Regional Science: Regional Research Institute, West Virginia University.* Retrieved March 14, 2009 from http://www.rri.wvu.edu/WebBook/Goetz/MIGXGLOS1.htm.

Gottschalk, Marie. (2006). *The Prison and the Gallows: The Politics of Mass Incarceration in America.* New York; Cambridge: Cambridge University Press.

Grasmick, Harold G., John K Cochran, Robert J. Bursik Jr., M'Lou Kimpel. (1993). "Religion, Punitive Justice, and Support for the Death Penalty." *Justice Quarterly.* 10.2. pp. 289-314.

Gray, Virginia, Russell L. Hanson, and Herbert Jacob. (1999). *Politics in the American States: A Comparative Analysis – 7ᵗʰ Edition.* Washington, D.C.: CQ Press.

Greenberg, Jack. (1986). "Against the American System of Capital Punishment." *Harvard Law Review.* 99:7. pp. 1670-1680.

Gregg v. Georgia. 428 U.S. 153 (1976). Retrieved November 7, 2007 from http://caselaw.lp.findlaw.com/scripts/getcase.pl?navby=CASE&court=US &vol=428&page=153.

Haddock, Geoffrey and Zanna, Mark P. (1998). "Assessing the Impact of Affective and Cognitive Information in Predicting Attitudes toward Capital Punishment." *Law and Human Behavior.* 22:3. pp. 325-339.

Hamm, Theodore. (2001). *Rebel and a Cause: Caryl Chessman and the Politics of the Death Penalty in Postwar California, 1948-1974.* Los Angeles and Berkeley, C.A.: University of California Press.

Haney, Craig. and D.D. Logan. 1994. "Broken Promise: The Supreme Court's Response to Social Science Research on Capital Punishment." *Journal of Social Issues.* 50:75-101

Haney, Craig, Hurtado, Aida, and Vega, Luis. (1994). "'Modern' Death Qualification: New Data on Its Biasing Effects." *Law and Human Behavior.* 18:6. pp. 619-633.

Haney, Craig. (1984)."Examining Death Qualification: Further Analysis of the Process Effect." *Law and Human Behavior.* 8:1/2. pp. 133-151.

Haney, Craig. (2005). *Death by Design: Capital Punishment as Social Psychological System.* Oxford; New York: Oxford University Press.

Harries, Keith and Derral Cheatwood. (1997). *The Geography of Execution: The Capital Punishment Quagmire of America.* Lanham, MD: Rowman & Littlefield Publishers, Inc.

Hartung, Frank E. (1952). "Trends in the Use of Capital Punishment." *Annals of the American Academy of Political and Social Science.* 284. pp. 8-19.

Harvard Law Review. (2001). "The Rhetoric of Difference and the Legitimacy of Capital Punishment." *Harvard Law Review.* 114:5. pp. 1599-1622.

Hochkammer, William O., Jr. (1969). "The Capital Punishment Controversy." *The Journal of Criminal Law, Criminology, and Police Science.* 60:3. pp. 360-368.

Huang, W. S. Wilson, Mary A. Finn, R. Barry Ruback, and Robert R. Friedmann, (1996). "Individual and Contextual Influences on Sentence Lengths: Examining Political Conservatism." *The Prison Journal.* 76. pp. 398–419.

In re Kemmler, 136 U.S. 436 (1889). Retrieved June 22, 2009 from http://supreme.justia.com/us/136/436/index.html.

Jackson, Jesse, Jr., Jackson, Jesse L., Sr., and Shapiro, Bruce. (2001). *Legal Lynching: The Death Penalty and America's Future.* New York: New Press, Distributed by W.W. Norton.

Jackson, Robert A. (1992). "Effects of Public Opinion and Political System Characteristics on State Policy Outputs." *Publius.* 22:4. pp. 31-46.

Jacobs, David and Jason T. Carmichael. (2004). "Ideology, Social Threat, and the Death Sentence: Capital Sentences Across Time and Space." *Social Forces.* 83:1. pp. 249-278.

Jacobs, David and Carmichael, Jason T. (2002). "The Political Sociology of the Death Penalty: A Pooled Time-Series Analysis." *American Sociological Review.* 67:1. pp. 109-131.

Jacobs, David and Jason T. Carmichael. (2001). "The Politics of Punishment across Time and Space: A Pooled Time-Series Analysis of Imprisonment Rates." *Social Forces.* 80:1. pp. 61-89. Retrieved May 13, 2009 from http://muse.jhu.edu/journals/social_forces/v080/80.1jacobs01.html.

Jacobs, David and Stephanie L. Kent. (2007). "The Determinants of Executions since 1951: How Politics, Protests, Public Opinion, and Social Divisions Shape Capital Punishment." *Social Problems.* 54:3, pp. 297–318. Retrieved August 13, 2008 from http://caliber.ucpress.net/doi/pdf/10.1525/sp.2007.54.3.297.

Jacobs, David, Jason T. Carmichael and Stephanie L. Kent. (2005). "Vigilantism, Current Racial Threat, and Death Sentences." *American Sociological Review.* 70: 4. pp. 656-677.

Jacobs, David. Zhenchao Qian, Jason T. Carmichael, and Stephanie L. Kent. (2007). "Who Survives on Death Row? An Individual and Contextual Analysis." *American Sociological Review.* 72: 4. pp. 610-632.

Jacoby, Joseph E. and Paternoster, Raymond. (1982). "Sentencing Disparity and Jury Packing: Further Challenges to the Death Penalty." *The Journal of Criminal Law and Criminology.* 73:1. pp. 379-387.

Johnson, Charles A. (1976). "Political Culture in American States: Elazar's Formulation Examined." *American Journal of Political Science.* 20:3. pp. 491-509.

Judges, Donald. P. (1999). Scared to Death: Capital Punishment as Authoritarian Terror Management. *University of California at Davis Law Review.* 33. pp. 155–248.

Jurek v. Texas 96 S.Ct. 2950 (1976). Retrieved November 24, 2007 from http://www.oyez.org/cases/1970-1979/1975/1975_75_5394/.

Karge, Stewart W. (1978). "Capital Punishment: Death for Murder Only." *The Journal of Criminal Law and Criminology.* 69:2. pp. 179-196.

Karp, David J. (1978). "Coker v. Georgia: Disproportionate Punishment and the Death Penalty for Rape." *Columbia Law Review.* 78:8. pp. 1714-1730.

Kennedy, Randall. (1998). "*McCleskey v. Kemp*: Race, Capital Punishment, and the Supreme Court." *Harvard Law Review.* 101: pp. 1388-1443.

King, Gilbert. (2008). *The Execution of Willie Francis: Race, Murder, and the Search for Justice in the American South.* New York, N.Y.: Basic Civitas Books

King, Ryan D. (2008). "Conservatism, Institutionalism, and the Social Control of Intergroup Conflict." *American Journal of Sociology.* 113:5. pp. 1351-1393.

Kingdon, John D. (2003). *Agendas, Alternatives, and Public Policies: 2nd Edition.* Reading, PA: Addison-Wesley Educational Publishers Inc.

Kronenwetter, Michael (2001). *Capital Punishment: A Reference Handbook – Second Edition.* Santa Barbara, CA: ABC-CLIO, Inc.

Layman, Geoffrey C. (1993). "Religion and Political Behavior: The Impact of Beliefs, Affiliations, and Commitment from 1980 to 1994." *The Public Opinion Quarterly.* 61:2. pp. 288-316.

Light, Alfred R. (1978). "Intergovernmental Sources of Innovation in State Administration." *American Politics Quarterly.* 6. pp. 147-65.

Lofquist, William S. (2001-2002). "Putting Them There, Keeping Them There, and Killing Them: An Analysis of State-Level Variations in Death Penalty Intensity." *Iowa Law Review.* 87. pp. 1505-1558.

Long, J. Scott and Freese, Jeremy. (2006). *Regression Models for Categorical Dependent Variables Using STATA: Second Edition.* College Station, TX: STATA Press.

Louisiana ex rel. Francis v. Resweber 329 U.S. 459 (1947). Retrieved November 24, 2007 from http://www.law.cornell.edu/supct/html/historics/USSC_CR_0329_0459_Z S.html.

Luginbuhl, James and Middendorf, Kathi. (1988). "Death Penalty Beliefs and Jurors' Responses to Aggravating and Mitigating Circumstances in Capital Trials." *Law and Human Behavior.* 12:3. pp. 263-281.

Lutz, James M. (1986). "The Spatial and Temporal Diffusion of Selected Licensing Laws in the United States." *Political Geography Quarterly.* 5. pp. 141-59.

Maryland Citizens Against State Executions (MD CASE). (2007). "History of the Death Penalty in Maryland." Retrieved February 15, 2008 from http://www.mdcase.org/node/20.

McAllister, Pam. (2003). *Death Defying: Dismantling the Execution Machinery in 21st Century U.S.A.* New York: Continuum.

McCann, Stewart J. H. (2008). "Societal Threat, Authoritarianism, Conservatism, and U.S. State Death Penalty Sentencing (1977-2004)." *Journal of Personality and Social Psychology.* 94:5. 913-923.

McCleskey v. Kemp 481 U.S. 279 (1987). Retrieved November 24, 2007 from http://www.law.umkc.edu/faculty/projects/ftrials/conlaw/mccleskey.html.

McIntyre, Allison. (2004) "Doctrine of Double Effect." *Stanford Encyclopedia of Philosophy.* Retrieved August 13, 2008 from http://plato.stanford.edu/entries/double-effect/.

McVoy, Edgar C. (1940). "Patterns of Diffusion in the United States." *American Sociological Review.* 5. pp. 219-27.

Meseaguer, Covadonga. (2005). "Policy Learning, Policy Diffusion, and the Making of a New Order." *The Annals of the American Academy of Political and Social Science.* 598. pp. 67-82. Retrieved May 14, 2009 from http://ann.sagepub.com/cgi/content/abstract/598/1/67.

Mill, John Stuart (1859). *On Liberty.* Copyright 1998 by The Pennsylvania State University. Retrieved October 17, 2008 from http://www2.hn.psu.edu/faculty/jmanis/jsmill/liberty.pdf.

Millemann, Michael A. and Gary W. Alexander. (2006). *Preferring White Lives: The Racial Administration of the Death Penalty in America.* Retrieved July 22, 2008 from http://ssrn.com/abstract=898645.

Miller, Kenneth W. and David Niven. (2009). *Death Justice: Rehnquist, Scalia, Thomas, and the Contradictions of the Death Penalty.* El Paso, TX: LFB Scholarly Publishing, LLC.

Miller v. Alabama (567 U. S. _____ (2012)). Retrieved April 14, 2014 from http://www.supremecourt.gov/opinions/11pdf/10-9646g2i8.pdf.

Minstrom, Michael. (1997). "Policy Entrepreneurs and the Diffusion of Innovation" *American Journal of Political Science.* 41:3. pp. 738-770. Retrieved May 13, 2009 from http://www.jstor.org/stable/2111674.

Mitchell, Michael and Jim Sidanius. (1995). "Social Hierarchy and the Death Penalty: A Social Dominance Perspective." *Political Psychology.* 16:3. pp. 591-619.

Mooney, Christopher Z. (2001). "Modeling Regional Effects on State Policy
 Diffusion." *Political Research Quarterly.* 54:1. pp. 103-124 Retrieved
 May 13, 2009 from http://www.jstor.org/stable/449210.

Mooney, Christopher Z. and Mei-Hsien Lee. (1995). "Legislating Morality in
 the American States: The Case of Pre-Roe Abortion Regulation Reform."
 American Journal of Political Science. 39:3, pp. 599-627.

Mooney, Christopher Z. and Mei-Hsien Lee. (1999a). "Morality Policy
 Reinvention: State Death Penalties." *Annals of the American Academy of
 Political and Social Science.* 566. pp. 80-92. Retrieved May 13, 2009 from
 http://www.jstor.org/stable/1048844.

Mooney, Christopher Z. and Mei-Hsien Lee. (1999b). "The Temporal
 Diffusion of Morality Policy: The Case of Death Penalty Legislation in the
 American States." *Policy Studies Journal.* 27:4. pp.766-780 Retrieved
 May 13, 2009 from http://www3.interscience.wiley.com/cgi-
 bin/fulltext/119072022/PDFSTART.

Morgan v. Illinois 504 US 719 (1992). Retrieved November 27, 2007 from
 http://caselaw.lp.findlaw.com/scripts/getcase.pl?court=US&vol=504&inv
 ol=719.

Mullin, Courtney. (1980). "The Jury System in Death Penalty Cases: A
 Symbolic Gesture." *Law and Contemporary Problems* 43:4. pp. 137-154.

Mwalili, Samuel M., Emmanuel Lesaffre, and Dominique Declerck. (2007).
 "The Zero-Inflated Negative Binomial Regression Model with Correction
 for Misclassification: An Example in Caries Research." *Statistical
 Methods in Medical Research.* 17. 123-139.

Nardulli, Peter F., Roy B. Fleming, and James Eisenstein. (1988). *The Tenor of
 Justice: Criminal Courts and the Guilty Plea Process.* Urbana, IL:
 University of Illinois Press.

National Association of Emergency Medical Technicians (NAEMT). (2006).
 *NAEMT Position Statement on EMT and Paramedic Participation in
 Capital Punishment.* Retrieved November 24, 2007 from
 http://www.naemt.org/aboutNAEMT/capitalpunishment.htm.

Newport, Frank. (2007). "Sixty-Nine Percent of Americans Support Death
 Penalty." *Gallup.* Retrieved April 28, 2012 from
 http://www.gallup.com/poll/101863/Sixtynine-Percent-Americans-
 Support-Death-Penalty.aspx.

Nice, David C. (1992). "The States and the Death Penalty." *The Western
 Political Quarterly.* 45:4. pp. 1037-1048.

Nisbett, Richard E. and Dov Cohen. (1996). *Culture of Honor: The Psychology of Violence in the South.* Boulder, Colorado: Westview Press.

Norrander, Barbara. (2000). "The Multi-Layered Impact of Public Opinion on Capital Punishment Implementation in the American States." *Political Research Quarterly.* 53:4. pp. 771-793.

Pardoe, Iain and Robert R. Weidner. (2004). "Sentencing Convicted Felons in the United States: A Bayesian Analysis Using Multilevel Covariates." *Journal of Statistical Planning and Inference.* 136. pp. 1433-1455.

Parenti, Christian. (1999). *Lockdown America: Police and Prisons in the Age of Crisis.* London, New York: Verso.

Paternoster, Raymond, Robert Brame, and Sarah Bacon. (2008). *The Death Penalty: America's Experience with Capital Punishment.* New York and Oxford: Oxford University Press.

Paternoster, Raymond, Robert Brame, Sarah Bacon, Andrew Ditchfield, David Biere, Karen Beckman, Deanna Perez, Michael Strauch, Nadine Frederique, Kristin Gawkoski, Daniel Zeigler, and Katheryn Murphy. (2003). *An Empirical Analysis of Maryland's Death Sentencing System with Respect to the Influence of Race and Legal Jurisdiction.* Retrieved November 22, 2007 from http://www.newsdesk.umd.edu/pdf/finalrep.pdf.

Patterson, E. Britt. (1991). "Poverty, Income Inequality, and Community Crime Rates." *Criminology.* 29:4. pp. 755-776. Retrieved May 19, 2009 from http://dx.doi.org/10.1111/j.1745-9125.1991.tb01087.x.

Patton v. State of Mississippi 332 U.S. 463 (1948). Retrieved November 24, 2007 from http://vlex.com/vid/20015920.

Peffley, Mark and Jon Hurwitz. (2007). "Persuasion and Resistance: Race and the Death Penalty in America." *American Journal of Political Science.* 51: 4. pp. 996-1012.

Penry v. Lynaugh 492 U.S. 302 (1989). Retrieved November 24, 2007 from http://www.oyez.org/cases/1980-1989/1988/1988_87_6177/.

Peterson, Ruth D. and Bailey, William C. (1988). "Murder and Capital Punishment in the Evolving Context of the Post-Furman Era." *Social Forces.* 66:3. pp. 774-807.

Phillips, Scott. (2008). "Racial Disparities in the Capital of Capital Punishment." *Houston Law Review.* 45. Retrieved August 19, 2008 from http://graphics8.nytimes.com/packages/pdf/national/20080429_sidebar_st udy.pdf.

Popper, Karl R. (1952). *The Open Society and Its Enemies. Vol. 1: The Spell of Plato*. Princeton: Princeton University Press.

Powell v. Alabama 287 U.S. 45 (1932). November 24, 2007 from http://caselaw.lp.findlaw.com/scripts/getcase.pl?court=US&vol=287&inv ol=45.

Proffitt v. Florida 96 S.Ct. 2960 (1976). Retrieved November 24, 2007 from http://www.law.cornell.edu/supct/html/historics/USSC_CR_0428_0242_Z S.html.

Radelet, Michael L. and Akers, Ronald L. (1996). "Deterrence and the Death Penalty: The Views of the Experts." *The Journal of Criminal Law and Criminology*. 87:1. pp. 1-16.

Radelet, Michael L. and Bedau, Hugo Adam. (1998). "The Execution of the Innocent." *Law and Contemporary Problems*. 61:4, pp. 105-124.

Radelet, Michael L. and Borg, Marian J. (2000). "The Changing Nature of Death Penalty Debates." *Annual Review of Sociology*. 26. pp. 43-61.

Rankin, Joseph H. (1979)."Changing Attitudes toward Capital Punishment." *Social Forces*. 58:1. pp. 194-211.

Reggio, Michael H. (1997). "History of the Death Penalty." *Society's Final Solution: A History and Discussion of the Death Penalty*. (Laura E. Randa, ed.). New York: University Press of America. Retrieved November 2, 2007 from http://www.pbs.org/wgbh/pages/frontline/shows/execution/readings/histor y.html.

Reiman, Jeffrey. (2004). *The Rich Get Richer and the Poor get Prison: Ideology, Class and Criminal Justice – 7th Edition*. Boston, MA: Allyn and Bacon.

Reynolds, Morgan O. (1977). "On Welfare Economics Aspects of Capital Punishment." *American Journal of Economics and Sociology*. 36: 1. pp. 105-109.

Roberts v. Louisiana 96 S.Ct. 3001 (1976). Retrieved November 24, 2007 from http://www.oyez.org/cases/1970-1979/1975/1975_75_5844/.

Robinson, Robert J. (1993). "What Does 'Unwilling' to Impose the Death Penalty Mean Anyway? Another Look at Excludable Jurors." *Law and Human Behavior*. 17:4. pp. 471-477.

Rogers, Alan. (1993). "'Under Sentence of Death': The Movement to Abolish Capital Punishment in Massachusetts, 1835-1849." *The New England Quarterly*. 66:1. pp. 27-46.

Roper v. Simmons (543 U.S. 551 (2005). Retrieved November 24, 2007 from http://www.law.cornell.edu/supct/html/03-633.ZS.html.

Rubin, Paul H., 2002. "The Death Penalty and Deterrence." *Phi Kappa Phi Forum*, Winter, v. 82, Issue 1, pp. 10-12.

Sarat, Austin and Christian Boulanger (eds). (2005). *Cultural Lives of Capital Punishment: Comparative Perspectives*. Stanford, CA : Stanford University Press.

Sarat, Austin. (1998). "Recapturing the Spirit of "Furman": The American Bar Association and the New Abolitionist Politics." *Law and Contemporary Problems*. 61:4. pp. 5-28.

Schaefer, Kristin D., James J. Hennessy, and Joseph G. Ponterotto. (2000). "Race as a Variable in Imposing and Carrying out the Death Penalty in the U.S." *Race, Ethnicity, Sexual Orientation, Violent Crime: The Realities and the Myths*. pp. 35-45. New York, London, Oxford: The Haworth Press, Inc.

Schneider, Anne and Helen Ingram. (1993). "Social Construction of Target Populations: Implications for Politics and Policy." *The American Political Science Review*. 87:2. pp. 334-347.

Schuessler, Karl F. (1952). "The Deterrent Influence of the Death Penalty." *Annals of the American Academy of Political and Social Science*. 284. pp. 54-62.

Simon, Rita J. and Dagny A. Blaskovich. (2002). *A Comparative Analysis of Capital Punishment: Statutes, Policies, Frequencies, and Public Attitudes the World Over*. Lanham, Boulder, New York, Oxford: Lexington Books.

Skipper v. South Carolina 476 U.S. 1 (1986). Retrieved November 24, 2007 from
http://vlex.com/vid/19975654.

Society of Correctional Physicians (SCP). (1997). "The SCP's Code of Ethics." Retrieved November 24, 2007 from
http://www.corrdocs.org/framework.php?pagetype=aboutethics&bgn=2.

Sorensen, Jon and Don Stemen. (2002). "The Effect of State Sentencing Policies on Incarceration Rates." *Crime Delinquency*. 48. pp. 456–475.

Sorenson, Jon, Robert Wrinkle, Victoria Brewer, and James Marquart. (1999). "Capital Punishment and Deterrence: Examining the Effect of Executions on Murder in Texas." *Crime and Delinquency*. 45:4, pp. 481-493.

Soss, Joe, Laura Langbein and Alan R. Metelko. (2003). "Why Do White Americans Support the Death Penalty?" *The Journal of Politics*. 65:2. pp. 397-421.

Statistical Consulting Group, UCLA Academic Technology Services. (2007). *Regression Models with Count Data.* Retrieved April 25, 2012 from http://www.ats.ucla.edu/stat/stata/seminars/count_presentation/count.htm.

Steiker, Carol S. and Steiker, Jordan M. (1995). "Sober Second Thoughts: Reflections on Two Decades of Constitutional Regulation of Capital Punishment." *Harvard Law Review.* 109:2. pp. 355-438.

Stevenson, Bryan and Friedman, Ruth. (1994). "Deliberate Indifference: Judicial Tolerance of Racial Bias in Criminal Justice." *Washington and Lee Law Review.* 51: 509-527.

Stream, Christopher. (1999). "Health Reform in the States: A Model of State Small Group Health Insurance Market Reforms." *Political Research Quarterly.* 52:3. pp. 499-526.

Stucky, Thomas D, Karen Heimer, and Joseph B. Lang. (2005). "Partisan Politics, Electoral Competition and Imprisonment: An Analysis of States Over Time." *Criminology.* 43:1. pp. 211-248. Retrieved May 12, 2009 from http://www3.interscience.wiley.com/cgi-bin/fulltext/118684107/PDFSTART.

Sutherland, E.H. (1950). "The Diffusion of Sexual Psychopath Laws." *American Journal of Sociology.* 56. pp.142-48.

Tabak, Ronald J. (1999). "Racial Discrimination in Implementing the Death Penalty." *American Bar Association: Section of Individual Rights and Responsibilities.* Retrieved November 22, 2007 from http://www.abanet.org/irr/hr/summer99/tabak.html.

The Free Dictionary. (2008). "Cruel and Unusual Punishment." Retrieved March 28, 2008 from http://www.thefreedictionary.com/cruel+and+unusual+punishment.

The Historical Society of Pennsylvania. (2008). "Glossary." Retrieved March 28, 2008 from http://www.hsp.org/default.aspx?id=644.

The Journal of Criminal Law and Criminology. (1976). "Capital Punishment." *The Journal of Criminal Law and Criminology.* 67:4. pp. 437-449.

The National Commission for the Protection of Human Subjects of Biomedical and Behavioral Research. (1979). *The Belmont Report.* Retrieved October 20, 2008 from http://ohsr.od.nih.gov/guidelines/belmont.html.

Thompson v. Oklahoma 108 S. Ct. 2687 (1987). Retrieved November 24, 2007 from http://www.oyez.org/cases/1980-1989/1987/1987_86_6169/.

Tolnay, Stewart E. and E. M. Beck. (1995). *A Festival of Violence: An Analysis of Southern Lynchings, 1882-1930*. Urbana, Chicago: University of Illinois Press.

Tropp v. Dulles 356 U.S. 86 (1958). Retrieved November 24, 2007 from http://www.law.cornell.edu/supct/html/historics/USSC_CR_0356_0086_Z O.html.

Turner v. Murray 476 U.S. 28 (1986). Retrieved November 24, 2007 from http://vlex.com/vid/19975660.

Tushnet, Mark. (1989). "Reflections on Capital Punishment: One Side of an Uncompleted Discussion." *Journal of Law and Religion.* 7:1. pp. 21-31.

Tyler, Tom R. and Renee Weber. (1982). Support for the Death Penalty: Instrumental Response to Crime, or Symbolic Attitude?" *Law & Society Review*. 17:1. pp. 21-45.

U. S. General Accounting Office. (1990). *Death Penalty Sentencing: Research Indicates Pattern of Racial Disparities*. Retrieved November 22, 2007 from http://archive.gao.gov/t2pbat11/140845.pdf.

U.S. Census Bureau. (2005). "Income Inequality (1947-1998)." Retrieved December 2, 2007 from http://www.census.gov/hhes/www/income/incineq/p60204/p60204txt.html.

U.S. Department of Justice, Bureau of Justice Statistics. (20011). "Capital Punishment 2010 – Statistical Tables." Retrieved April 24, 2012 from http://www.bjs.gov/content/pub/pdf/cp10st.pdf.

U.S. Legal Definitions. (2008a) "Mental Illness Law and Legal Definition." Retrieved May 20, 2009 from http://definitions.uslegal.com/m/mental-illness/.

U.S. Legal Definitions. (2008b) "Mental Retardation Law and Legal Definition." Retrieved May 20, 2009 from http://definitions.uslegal.com/m/mental-retardation/.

Unah, Isaac and Jack Boger. (2001). "Race and the Death Penalty in North Carolina: An Empirical Analysis: 1993-1997." *Death Penalty Information Center*. Retrieved August 19, 2008 from http://www.deathpenaltyinfo.org/article.php?did=246&scid=.

Unnever, James D. and Francis T. Cullen. (2005). "Executing the Innocent and Support for Capital Punishment: Implications for Public Policy." *Criminology & Public Policy*. 4:1. pp. 3-38.

Unnever, James D. and Francis T. Cullen. (2007). "The Racial Divide in Support for the Death Penalty: Does White Racism Matter?" *Social Forces*. 85:3. pp. 1281-1301.

Unnever, James D., Francis T. Cullen and Cheryl Lero Johnson. (2008). "Race, Racism, and Support for Capital Punishment." *Crime and Justice*. 37. pp. 45-96.

Van Hiel, Alain and Ivan Mervielde. (2002). "Explaining Conservative Beliefs and Political Preferences: A Comparison of Social Dominance Orientation and Authoritarianism." *Journal of Applied Social Psychology*. 32:5. pp. 965-976.

Wacquant, Loic. (1999). "France: US Exports Zero Tolerance." *Le Monde*. Translated by Tarik Wareh. Retrieved February 25, 2008 from http://www.mapinc.org/drugnews/v99/n466/a06.html.

Wacquant, Loic. (2001a). "The Advent of the Penal State is Not a Destiny." *Social Justice*. 28:3. pp. 81-87.

Wacquant, Loic. (2001b). "The Penalisation of Poverty and the rise of Neo-Liberalism." *European Journal on Criminal Policy and Research*. 9:4. pp. 401-412.

Wacquant, Loic. (2003). "Toward a Dictatorship Over the Poor." *Punishment and Society: The International Journal of Penology*. 5:2. pp. 197-205.

Wainwright v. Witt 477 U.S. 168 (1985). Retrieved November 27, 2007 from http://caselaw.lp.findlaw.com/scripts/getcase.pl?court=US&vol=477&inv ol=168.

Walker, Jack L. (1969). "The Diffusion of Innovations among the American States." *The American Political Science Review*. 63:3. pp. 880-899. Retrieved May 14, 2009 from http://www.jstor.org/stable/1954434.

Weems v. U.S. 217 U.S. 349 (1910). Retrieved November 24, 2007 from http://vlex.com/vid/20027174.

Weidner, Robert R. and Richard S. Frase. (2001). "A County-Level Comparison of the Propensity to Sentence Felons to Prison." *International Journal of Comparative Criminology*. 1. pp. 1–22.

Weidner, Robert R. and Richard S. Frase. (2003). "Legal and Extralegal Determinants of Intercounty Differences in Prison Use." *Criminal Justice Policy Review*. 14:3. pp. 377-400.

Weisbuch, Jonathan B. (1984). "The Public Health Effects of the Death Penalty." *Journal of Public Health Policy*. 5:3. pp. 305-311.

Western, Bruce. (2006). *Punishment and Inequality in America*. New York: Russell Sage Foundation.

Wilkerson v. Utah 99 U.S. 130 (1878). Retrieved November 24, 2007 from http://supreme.justia.com/us/99/130/.

Witherspoon v. Illinois 391 U.S. 510 (1968). Retrieved November 24, 2007 from http://supreme.justia.com/us/391/510/case.html.

Woodson v. North Carolina 96 S. Ct. 2978 (1976). Retrieved November 24, 2007 from http://www.oyez.org/cases/1970-1979/1975/1975_75_5491/.

Wright, Gerald C., Robert S. Erikson, and John P. McIver. (1985). "Measuring State Partisanship and Ideology with Survey Data." *Journal of Politics.* 47:2. pp. 469-489.

Young, Robert L. (1991). "Race, Conceptions of Crime and Justice, and Support for the Death Penalty." *Social Psychology Quarterly.* 54:1. pp. 67-75.

Young, Robert L. (1992). "Religious Orientation, Race and Support for the Death Penalty." *Journal for the Scientific Study of Religion.* 31:1. pp. 76-87.

Zeisel, Hans. (1976). "The Deterrent Effect of the Death Penalty: Facts v. Faiths." *The Supreme Court Review.* 1976. pp. 317-343.

Zimmerman, Paul R. (2006). "Estimates of the Deterrent Effect of Alternative Execution Methods in the United States: 1978–2000." *American Journal of Economics and Sociology.* 65:4. pp. 909-941.

Zimmers, Teresa A.; Sheldon, Jonathan; Lubarsky, David A.; Lopez-Munoz, Francisco; Waterman, Linda; Weisman, Richard; Koniaris, Leonidas G. (2007). "Lethal Injection for Execution: Chemical Asphyxiation?" *PloS Medicine.* 4:4. Retrieved October 5, 2007 from http://medicine.plosjournals.org/perlserv/?request=get-document&doi=10.1371%2Fjournal.pmed.0040156.

Zimring, Franklin E. (2004). *The Contradictions of American Capital Punishment.* New York: Oxford University Press.

Index